Sidelines & Pearls:

A 50-Year Perspective on
the Lives of Coaches' Wives

by

Erica Barnett

Published by SuburbanBuzz.com LLC

Cover photos by Dave Sanders, Fulshear, Texas

ISBN-13: 978-1986271684
ISBN-10: 1986271684

Dedication

This book is written to honor the memory of my grandmother, who was a coach's wife for 44 "official" years but dedicated more than 50 years in total to the nurturing of coaches' wives. She was an original unsung treasure who blazed the trail for the rest of us. You'll find her wit and wisdom sprinkled throughout each chapter.

Elizabeth Ann "Betty" Frey Wasserman
July 1, 1939- May 29, 2017

Wife to Lloyd Wassermann

Mother of Mark James Wassermann
Linda Suzanne Wassermann
Stacey Lynn Wassermann
Randall James Wassermann

Table of Contents

Foreward
by Susan Rodgers

I've read several books written by coaches' wives, but it isn't every day that I've seen one span 50 years. Going back to those early days (before there was a "how to" guide) really shows the pioneering efforts of women like Betty Wassermann.

Betty married a young head coach when she was just 19 years old and dove straight into the world of coaching. It was sink or swim … and she swam! Her husband, Lloyd, could not have asked for a better partner. She was selfless, supportive, and set the standard for her peers—those in her heyday and those married to coaches today. This was years before the American Football Coaches Wives Association was formed. I remember joining the AFCWA and wondering how coaches' wives managed to function a generation earlier. The answer is, they managed thanks to strong and generous mentors like Betty.

Betty passed away May of 2017, leaving behind insights that her granddaughter, Erica Barnett, shares on each page. Erica is one of those legacy kids who grew up around football and knew more about it as a youngster than most adults. It's no surprise she became a sports journalist and married a high school football coach. I'm happy our paths intersected and that we share an interesting personal connection. Erica's relative, Drew Brees, is a dear friend of my youngest son Jonny. Drew wrote about this friendship and their days at Westlake High (in Austin) in Coming Back Stronger, one of Drew's many books. Obviously, creativity runs in Erica's extended family, for another cousin, Michael Waxman, directed the television series Friday Night Lights. How wonderful that her inspiration comes from her family tree, the sidelines, the field, television, and books written by her relatives!

Like Erica, I began my "coach's wife" career by marrying a high school coach. I was a teacher, and at that time Randy Rodgers was a dashing specimen of athleticism and sportsman-ship. He's now a veteran of more than 35 years in the college recruiting arena. As a major college coach and Division 1 Recruiting Coordinator, he brings his own unique "Texas" perspective to the college recruiting process. Together we raised our three remarkable boys, two who segued into the NFL and coached for the Chicago Bears. Our eldest, Jay, is a defensive line coach. Jeff, our middle child, was the special teams coordinator. It's rare for siblings to coach on the same NFL team, but it certainly made it easier for Randy and me to attend games and cheer them on! Jeff is now with the Arizona Cardinals as the Special Teams Coordinator, so it will be different this year going to two different teams. It's a good problem to have.

This, and more, is what makes being a coach's wife so incredibly meaningful. We never know the twists and turns life will bring. What we do know is that we are proud of our coach-husbands, our coach-sons, and the players. Coaches and their wives impact hundreds of young men in such profound ways. I recall that when our sons were young, we couldn't afford official babysitters. Sometimes the football players babysat for us, and now they are 45 to 50 years old. The stories they tell at reunions about "babysitting for the coach" are quite funny!

So enjoy this book, written from the lens of what was, what is, and what has remained "evergreen" in our roles as coaches' wives and coaches' mothers.

Acknowledgments

First and foremost, I thank my husband, Jeffrey Barnett, for his strong support of my sports journalism career and this book. Although some describe the profession of coaching as "selfish," he still finds ways to encourage me, inspire others, and make a difference in this world. He sacrifices so much while pursuing his calling and supporting the family he loves. It is amazing to see him in action on the field, but even more so as a husband and father. Watching him with our newborn Noah is truly heart melting, and I hope and pray our son grows up to be a "chip off the old block." I'm so proud of Jeffrey as an entrepreneur and the developer of a foot-ball app—and I have no idea how he manages to balance all these moving parts. One thing I do know, however, is that he is fully invested in his players and wants nothing more than for them to grow into upstanding citizens, with the powerful influence of teamwork as their foundation. Without a doubt, Jeffrey is the love of my life, and I am so deeply honored to journey through the world of coaching arm-in-arm with this incredible man.

I want to thank my grandfather, "PaPa" Lloyd Wassermann, for planting our family legacy in 1961. He graduated from Texas A&M at the age of 19, immediately married my "MiMi" Betty Frey, and began a career as an all-sport coach, head coach, athletic coordinator, athletic director, and assistant principal. People fondly called him "Lord" Wassermann and "Bear" for a reason— Bear Bryant was his coach at A&M, and he was John David Crow's full back. He inspired players, parents, peers, administrators, and fans with his decency, intensity, focus on academics, love of all sports, and most of all his faith. Seven of his athletes played in the NFL. He retired as a coach and educator after 44 years and was inducted into the Brenham High School Hall of Honor. Then PaPa ran for Brazos County Commissioner and served three terms (12 years). That's a total of 56 years in the workforce before he permanently retired in December 2016. He inspired the best in us all—his children, grandchildren, and one great-grandchild. Most importantly, he loved and credited my "MiMi" for her steadfastness and excellence in the role of a coach's wife.

Betty Frey Wassermann was a classic coach's wife and the best MiMi a granddaughter could ever ask for. She loved us all and was such an example of grace and dignity. I lost much more than a grandmother at her passing in May of 2017—I lost a mentor, supporter, and confi-dante. I am a better version of coach's wife today because of her advice. Her "pearls of wisdom" inspired the title of my Sidelines & Pearls website and business. She really blazed the trail for coaches' wives in all sports spanning half a century, but it was her insights into the football culture that especially impacted me. She is the muse behind this book—a guide into our lifestyle. Her narrative spans 50 years and is a primer on the secret lives of coaches' wives. This book is filled with "gifts" from this remarkable women: ethics that guided her demeanor, good judgment from an intelligent brain and compassionate heart, and intestinal fortitude as she shouldered various responsibilities such as wife, mother, employee, volunteer, and support system for a sisterhood of coaches' wives. She battled multiple illnesses bravely and had an unshakeable faith. If you have days when you wonder how you'll manage it all, just look to MiMi as an example.

My mother, Linda "Suzanne" Wassermann, is a constant in my life, my siblings' lives, PaPa's life, and the life of my son Noah. I'm not sure what I'd do without her. I believe she was raised differently "on purpose" to be independent, responsible, competitive, and athletic in an era when girls were often encouraged to be just the opposite. I was fortunate to be shaped and molded by a highly creative, artistic mother whose interior design, custom furniture, and wall finishing work has appeared in Ladies' Home Journal and Builder Magazine. More impressive is her athletic ability—track, cross country, basketball, softball, tennis, cheer leading, competition twirl, and a dance background. With that pedigree, is it any wonder that I work in the world of sports journalism?

A sincere and enthusiastic "thank you" to the remarkable coaches' wives who contributed their wise, insightful and often humorous voices to this book, including (in alphabetical order):

Janice Archer, wife of Coach Don Archer

Kristin Antill Bourgeois, wife of Coach Jason Bourgeois

Rhonda Clayton, wife of Coach Don Clayton

Robin Cook, wife of Coach Lee Cook

Lois Faigle, wife of Coach Jerry Faigle

Lisa Gotte, wife of Coach BJ Gotte

Jordan Harrell, wife of Coach Clark Harrell

Ellie Mallory, wife of Coach Bill Mallory

Lisa Mallory, wife of Coach Doug Mallory

Susan Rodgers, wife of Coach Randy Rodgers

Julie West, wife of Coach Glenn West

Shirley West (in memoriam), wife of Coach Kenneth West

A big "thank you" to the coaches' kids who contributed their insights, including Paige Thurmond, Emily Mallory, Allison Mallory, Gretchen West and Gracie West.

Many thanks to Dusty Vandenberg, who added his insights as a high school football player who was impacted by the kindness of several coaches' wives.

A special thanks, as well, to those who posted on social media in memory of my grand-mother. There are too many to list in total, but I wanted to note the kind words of Teresa Combe, Lauri

Corbelli, and Gordon Ray LeBlanc.

A shout out to SuburbanBuzz.com Publishing and my editor, Melanie Saxton, who worked with me through my late-term contractions, interviewed many of the book's contributors, and found the magic in my memories.

Introduction

"She's not just my #1 fan. She's the glue."
~ Coach Jeffrey Barnett

Behind every great coach stands a great coach's wife. This is definitely true. You may not see us, but we are there. We've been there since sports were invented and high school foot-ball became a "thing," especially in Texas.

Yes, Texas high school football is a legend unto itself (more on that later). But regardless of where you live or what sport your husband is involved in, we love our coaches and are proud of them. It takes a lot of hard work to become a great coach's wife. I come from a line of coaches' wives (and the men they love), but even I'm thrown for a loop now and then. Thank heavens for my grandmother, fondly referred to as MiMi. She was a coach's wife for 44 years and involved in the coaching culture for well over 50 years. Just imagine the wisdom she shared with women who became engaged or newly married to a coach—me included!

We lost her in May of 2017, and I'm honored to capture her essence in each chapter. It's a multi-layered manuscript—a primer covering timeless principles and a fresh look at what a modern wife faces daily. It's a meaningful way for me "pay it forward," as my MiMi always encouraged me to do. MiMi and her peers (many whom contributed to this book) watched as the world of sports changed over time, but steadfastly advised that duty and dedication are eternal. This book is filled with her insights and those of other notable coaches' wives as a resource for newly engaged, the newly married, and the veterans of our crazy coaching culture.

So what was MiMi's secret to success? She believed in squeezing the most out of every moment spent with her busy coaching husband, and this led to a happy, productive pairing. This is major, and I mean major, because those who marry into the profession will soon learn how fleeting the moments of togetherness are. That's part of the culture shock—learning how to be a reasonably happy wife with an absent husband. But never fear! Learning the ropes doesn't happen overnight, but it will happen. It's a slow learning process that you can master with a pinch of patience and that all-important dash of duty. You'll see what I mean as you turn the pages.

For brand new and unacclimated wives, I compare marrying a coach to moving to another country. You're suddenly immersed in a foreign culture and find that you must learn a new language. The new language is called X's and O's and fluency is recommended to survive day-to-day discussions. This means you'll need to master the numbers that go along with each X and O. As the seasons change, the numbers change. When you take time to learn the basic patterns of the language, you can quite possibly become an expert and spot penalties or errors.

Besides the language, you'll learn a new time schedule. Fall, winter, summer, and spring become preseason, season, and off-season. There are the playoffs, which often intermingle with the holidays.

Of course, there is one advantage to each new season. Instead of having a summer and winter wardrobe, we now accumulate spirit-themed clothing for every occasion. Looking for a color that will flatter you? FORGET IT! My wardrobe consists of the basic school colors. And it never fails that when you change schools, the color is never the same. Just try dying "kelly green" to maroon. However, the simplicity of t-shirts, jerseys, and comfy jeans is worth it. Of course, every once in a while I see some "bleachers and bling" attire that makes me go online and order something sparkly. I once saw a rhinestone-adorned t-shirt emblazoned with The Toughest Part of The Game is Being the Coach's Wife, and really thought that was awesome.

After you know the language and adjust to a new schedule, it's time to toughen the skin. Yes, thick skin is essential, especially when you love your husband to the moon. This was my most challenging adjustment, and it has taken years to develop. I still struggle with it. You see, the verbal abuse heaped upon coaches ranks only next to the President our country. It's painful to watch, even from the sidelines. At times you'll be tempted to "school" the fair-weather fans and set the record straight. You might even be tempted to sit on the visitor's side because it's much easier to witness the abuse of enemies rather than your coach.

You will not be the only wife who has this problem. But when you toughen up, you'll be able to sit calmly in the midst of the pitchforks and burning torches verbal assaults and realize it does not matter, because you know your man is the greatest coach on the planet!

If you have adjusted so far, you are nearly there! Now it is time to emotionally accept sports. The old saying "It's not whether you win or lose ..." is a bunch of hogwash, especially when you share a home with the winner or loser. Some have no idea what is like to LIVE football, basketball, baseball or other sports every day, even during the "myth" of the off-season. Those trite words, "The thrill of victory and the agony of defeat," become your personal anthem from week to week.

Is it worth it all? YOU BET!

I would not trade places with any other wife for anything in the world. Where else can you witness the ultimate high of instilling pride in the heart of a 15-18-year-old student athlete? Hearing the words, "Did you see me, Coach? I DID IT!" creates moments and memories you'll treasure for a lifetime.

When you sit in the stands or stand on the sidelines (my normal spot), either yelling your head off or keeping to yourself, you might be asked, "Do you have someone playing?" I proudly smile and respond, "Yep, he's the one in the coach's uniform." I love my coach and am so proud of everything he masters on the playing field, but more importantly, off the playing field.

So buckle up for a roller coaster of highs and lows—and insights across a 50-year arc—and trust that you'll eventually enjoy the ride. So many wonderful coaches' wives, coaches' moms, and coaches' kids (and one former football player) contributed to this book, which was written to remind us all that we are not alone. As for newer wives, you'll be a savvy member of our sisterhood in no time!

Chapter 1: Dos, Don'ts and Duty

The requirements of coaching football are many, but there's a clear unsung hero—the wife.
~ Coach Lloyd Wassermann

I'm a proud coach's wife from a family tree with many branches of coaches, coaches' wives, athletes, and sports creatives in the entertainment industry. Actually, football runs on both sides, and my husband calls it my pedigree. But it's really a family legacy built on hard work and faith. I thank my lucky stars that I was born into the mighty Texas high school and college football tradition (more about that in the teamwork chapter). It prepared me for life as a coach's wife, although I had no inkling back then that I'd meet and marry Jeffrey Barnett and usher our son into the same culture.

The truth is, as coaches' wives our role today is very much like it was half a century ago when my grandmother, Betty Wassermann, married a coach. This first chapter, and the book itself, is a portal into her world, past and present. I think it proves that the more things change, the more things stay the same, especially when it comes to *do*s, *don't*s and duty.

My grandmother's wedding occurred just after my grandfather, Lloyd Wassermann, graduated from college at the tender age of 19, which was an accomplishment in itself. You heard that right ... he graduated from *college* as a teenager. My grandmother (MiMi), who was a teenager herself, became an instant head coach's wife and quickly learned that the profession is a 24/7/365-day-a-year undertaking. This perfect pair was so young. The pressure was intense, as you can imagine. But MiMi was born for the role—a role that officially lasted 44 years until my grandfather retired, and was extended unofficially for more than 50 years due to the presence of sports, football, and coaching in our family and friendship dynamics.

Even in the off-season, my grandfather (PaPa) prepared for the next year, recruited, went to clinics, and made sure athletes handled their grades and stayed in shape. This was an era when film was airdropped onto the football field—well before the advent of the Internet and digital conveniences. He loved working in the world of coaching—one he calls a selfish profession balanced by MiMi's selflessness. She was his universe. He is the first to say that the requirements of coaching football are many, but there's a clear unsung hero—the wife. MiMi was that wife. She was always present, even when he wasn't. She was calm, even when he wasn't. The demands of coaching, then and now, forge strong women who singlehandedly run households, coordinate schedules, raise children, transport the family, feed guests, deflect critics, and emotionally support the public figures they are married to.

MiMi also witnessed the role of women change over the years. As women entered universities and the workforce, they found themselves juggling it all—careers on top of family, households, and all the extra responsibilities that came with being married to a coach. Some wives became coaches themselves, or educators, counselors, doctors, and lawyers.

***

Within this book, I share multiple insights from MiMi's dear friends who walked the same path, such as Janice Archer, wife of Coach Don Archer; Robin Cook, wife of Coach Lee Cook; and Lois Faigle, wife of Coach Jerry Faigle. These were among her closest friends, who weigh in with observations about MiMi's leadership in an era when official support groups were rare or nonexistent.

Many notable coaches' wives knew my grandmother, and some ran in the same circles, such as Shirley West (in memoriam), wife of Kenneth West; Julie West, wife of Coach Glenn West; Susan Rodgers, wife of Coach Randy Rodgers; and Ellie Mallory, wife of Coach Bill Mallory. These women became trailblazers in their own right, some as founding members of coaches' wives organizations.

Other remarkable wives also contributed within these pages, such as Lisa Mallory, wife of Coach Doug Mallory; Kristin Antill Bourgeois, wife of Coach Jason Bourgeois; Rhonda Clayton, wife of Coach Don Clayton; Lisa Gotte, wife of Coach BJ Gotte; and Jordan Harrell, wife of Coach Clark Harrell. These perspectives are eye-opening and include NFL to collegiate to high school coaching adventures while raising children and moving from state to state! You'll see me refer to all these distinguished coaches' wives time and again in this and the following chapters.

I think all would agree with MiMi that there are four basic "evergreen" components to being a coach's wife, no matter if you are a millennial or vintage version:

1.) Find a support system or become one

2.) Be kind and inclusive to other wives

3.) Be discreet and thick-skinned

4.) Keep your husband healthy

Support System

MiMi's first "do" (or piece of advice) is to have a support system. Several books on Amazon have been written to help coaches walk the minefield of picking teams, dealing with parents, and keeping up in a fast-paced, competitive profession. Carl Pierson authored *The Politics of Coaching*. John M. Barry wrote *Power Plays: Politics, Football, and Other Blood Sports*. Jim Nantz wrote the New York Times bestseller *Toughness*. There are books for coach's wives as well, like Janis B. Meredith's *Coach's Wife Survival Guide: 22 Ways to Help Your Husband be a Winning Coach* and Carolyn Allen's *The Coach's Wife: The Feelings, Pressures, and Triumphs of Life with a Coach* (one of my favorites).

But guess what? No one has written a "coaches' wives book" with multiple perspectives honed over 50 years and passed down through the generations. In fact, a few of MiMi's friends offer insights that go back as far as the 60s, 70s, and 80s. That's A LOT of life spent under the microscope. And with my grandmother's recent passing, it seems even more appropriate to share the wit, wisdom, and whimsy that defined her life and prepared me to become Jeffrey's wife—a football spouse, mother, and granddaughter who became inspired to write this primer in my grandmother's honor.

Lots of women who were not raised around football, then and now, have no clue about the vernacular. So MiMi explained the offensive roles of the quarterback, tailback/halfback, fullback, wide receiver, center, guard, tackle, tight end, as well as the defensive roles of the end, middle linebacker, outside linebacker, cornerback, free safety, and strong safety. Whew! For those of you still learning to speak the language, I've put a glossary of terms and some deeper explanations in the back of the book. Flip there to brush up on your lingo so you can answer questions from the bleachers. You can bet people will lean on you to explain the game.

"Wait a minute...the safety is both a player and a play?" they'll ask, so the glossary is a good start.

Within these pages, I share my family's sports and filmmaking legacy that led to my career as a sports journalist, vlogger, and entrepreneur. But MiMi inspired me to do more. She listened as I brainstormed and envisioned a modern-day online coaches' wives support system with insights, tips, and encouragement. The notion certainly took off! What's so cool is that my core audience is coach's wives from all parts of the country who feel comfortable enough to give advice, take advice, and support each other on multiple virtual platforms. My own mantra is: *We Wives Shall Stick Together!* That's why I've rolled out the Ultimate Forum to talk about everything involved in being the wife of a coach (active or inactive), from Little League, to professional sports, to retirement.

I share other coaches' wives blogs as well and learn from women of all walks of life. Yes, I'm blessed by the warmth and honesty of these wonderful wives every single day. When I'm down, this online sisterhood is there for me. When they're down, I'm there for them. A post might read: *If your coach is coaching, if your kiddos are playing, and if you're having to do it all today ... just remember we are ALL thinking about you and wish you the happiest of days!* Another post might say: *Act like a lady, scream like a coach's wife!* Little pick-me-ups are priceless, and that's precisely the way it is supposed to be. It's a "MiMi-approved" social media following—honest and real. This incredible audience is another inspiration for this book, by the way.

In fact, I hope you'll join our strong coalition—17k followers on Twitter, 24k on Instagram, and the Evolve With Erica Snap Chat with more than 5k plus views daily. Facebook is hopping also with several Sidelines & Pearls groups and a fan page. All of these platforms are continually growing, and there is no better hands-on, authentic digital "sorority" than those within these groups. Check out sidelinesandpearls.com website for podcasts and articles covering the sports we all love, as well.

If ever there was a time to share a book with a cross-section of the wives' perspectives, it's now! After all, these women have maintained successful marriages (and their sanity) in an increasingly difficult landscape. And by reading this book, you'll share in the enduring messages of coaches' wives past and present—straight from the heart and written "just for us" as we juggle and struggle and celebrate our crazy lives.

Kindness and Inclusion

Do be kind and inclusive to fellow wives. MiMi was an enthusiastic and generous mentor. PaPa was famous for his high school and college coaching resume, while MiMi was famous for being genuinely gracious. She guided her peers (and me) through the physical, mental, emotional and spiritual fallout, as well as the thrill of victory. The assistant coaches' wives looked up to her. She blazed the trail and is remembered for helping other women transition into the world of coaching, with all its inherent joys and sorrows.

Her legacy, more than anything else, was an ability to diffuse awkward situations and welcome newbies with open arms. Those were genteel times—the wives threw tea parties and dressed up for each occasion. It was a bit less casual than our jeans and jerseys wardrobes of today. There was a greater emphasis on manners, and decorum was a part of everyday life. Someone had to teach the ins and outs of "graciousness," and that someone was MiMi. Coaching staffs were smaller, and everyone interacted in person. Without the buffer of the Internet, email and smart phones, all that was left were face-to-face encounters.

There was no such thing as "impersonal" acquaintances. There was no such thing as "clicks" or "mean girls" or "uncharitable attitudes." Individual families grew into large "coaching families" with bonds that lasted generations. They were there for each other, win, lose or draw. One good example is Janice Archer, a dear friend of my grandparents. Her husband Don coached for PaPa, and she commented that the Wassermann home was always open:

"We faced a lot of challenges as coaches' wives and had each other as friends, a close-knit group that at times traveled together to go to out-of-town football games. Don was not a varsity coach, but Betty was always good about checking with me to see if I'd like to ride along. I was always included on plans—all the wives were included, and that's what made Betty so special. I remember she had a station wagon, and we'd load the kids in the back. She made sure there were seats for us all, and after these games we got together. We all took turns providing food and fellowship, win or lose."

***

Today, the social atmosphere is sometimes different, meaning it's either friendly and inclusive, or it's not. Life is so complicated in this online, electronic age. Marriages and jobs are complicated like no other time in history. So in general, we relocate from town to town and hope for the best. As a coach's wife, you deal with the luck of the draw. We may land smack dab in the middle of an extended family, or we might find ourselves in a group that is less than accepting.

From day one after marrying PaPa, MiMi was a head coach's wife—and back then head coaches dealt with ALL the sports on top of teaching. At most, MiMi was part of a seven-woman pack. But today, a head coach's wife might have more than a dozen wives under her wing, depending on how many sports are involved. So, there are baseball coaches' wives, basketball coaches' wives, track coaches' wives, swim coaches' wives, tennis coaches' wives, and so on. This is a huge undertaking for head coaches' wives, who are generally looked to for leadership and support.

The truth is, the head coach's wife often determines how inclusive a group is. It's a huge job. If she welcomes and encourages and supports new wives (and all wives), it creates a vibrant atmosphere and makes functioning in the culture just a bit easier. If she doesn't, you may face a click or ~~cluster of dark forces~~ unfriendly faces. No coach's wife should bring unnecessary or hurtful challenges to the other wives, and MiMi really got that. But today, the subtle or not-so-subtle "freezing out," "bashing," and making others feel "lesser than" may occur on cellular group messages and private gossip groups on Facebook. MiMi noticed. She believed this behavior was beneath the dignity of a head coach's wife or any coach's wife, and blamed a lot of it on poor upbringing. To her dying breath, she believed that coaches' wives should be 100% united, regardless of who works at home, from home, or outside the home.

***

And so my own mantra is (a blunt but truthful mantra, by the way): I believe in my ability to stay positive and protect myself from 1.) people who are negative, 2.) people who drop mental trash in my environment, and 3.) "can't-do" people. This is the biggest contribution to my family I can make. If you want bigger things, have a bigger attitude and get everyone close to you on the same page. Nothing good can happen when you involve yourself in non-positive relationships.

Discretion

The sport of football has evolved. But although today's technology is light-years advanced, the duties of a coach's wife are basically the same. The "*dos*" and "*don'ts*" are the same. Human nature is the same. The politics are the same. And navigating the personalities is the same. Coaches' wives interact with parents, students, athletes, booster clubs, parent-teacher organizations, alumni, administrations, and fans ... and all of these "forces" have opinions. Some have quite vocal opinions that may not always be favorable.

MiMi knew a lot about human nature and even more about the fickle nature of acclaim. When it came to public reaction and group gossip, is it any surprise that her best advice, delivered ever so politely, was always, "Smile, keep your mouth closed, and walk away." The bottom line is that I represent and support my husband, and it's his opinion that matters. Poor conduct on my part will only hurt his career, and I keep this in mind at all times. Plus, MiMi always encouraged other coach's wives to support their husbands by steering clear of politics. I keep far away from conversations that can be misinterpreted, misconstrued, re-interpreted, or twisted into something negative.

A great example of "misinterpretation" is shared by Eleanor "Ellie" Mallory, wife of Coach Bill Mallory and mother of three coaches: Mike Mallory of the Jaguars, Doug Mallory of the Falcons, and Curt Mallory of Indiana State. Ellie was a founding member of the American Football Coaches' Wives Association (AFCWA) and served as the first and second-year president. Today she's on the Board of Trustees.

"When Bill was first coaching at the college level, the students didn't have the type of academic support they have today, such as departments devoting to tutoring. Bill had a few players who needed some help with course work, and he'd send them to our house. I would help them study and research. This was in in August, a time of year when coaches get tuned up for the season, leaving early in the morning and returning very late at night.

A librarian moved in next door to us and never saw Bill, but she DID see players come in and out of the house. I wondered why she wasn't being very friendly …

At this time, I and some other women were involved in situational role playing and would demonstrate how different scenarios can be construed from different viewpoints. The Methodist church invited us to perform. When I was introduced, guess who was in the audience? Yes, my neighbor, the librarian. She stood up and said, 'Well I didn't know she was married' in reference to the students coming in and out of my house. The audience didn't know what to do! I said, 'I'm very married' and realized just how easy it is for people to jump to conclusions, especially when they don't understand the coaching life!"

***

Discretion involves being able to deal with very vocal opinions. Some fans on the bleachers don't think twice about talking smack until the next win. This is hard on the coach, the wife who loves him, and his children. Sometimes I want to say, *"C'mon, people, my heart is on that field!"* After overhearing something totally snide and judgmental, I have to check myself so I don't react, retaliate, or do something I'll regret later. I have to watch myself on social media too. Remember, the Internet is forever. An indiscreet wife may open her mouth and insert foot, offending very important people who won't hire her husband because she's now perceived as a liability.

Although I was raised with the mindset of discretion, I still do not have MiMi's thick skin. That's something that has to toughen on its own. Take, for instance, a tweet by Coach Gene Chizik of Iowa State, Auburn University, and the University of North Carolina at Chapel Hill. By the way, he married Jonna, the daughter of his high school football coach, which is why I follow him on social media. Here's his take on team bashing:

"Everybody who enters the coaching profession knows the deal. Produce, or get fired. It's just that simple. But for all fans who hide behind keyboards & smear coaches, you're not just ripping coaches apart. You're ripping wives and children apart, too. #keyboardcowards #CFB."

***

Sometimes it's not easy to keep out of the sticky traps. No matter what city I live in, I wake up every day, put smile on my face, enjoy the game, and show up for social functions. Not only do I have to learn group dynamics, I also have to learn the "etiquette" of escape plans. You have to mentally prepare to back out of a room without it being obvious.

My reaction to any negativity is to seek out happiness, or create it myself online. There are thousands and thousands of coaches' wives throughout the nation, each looking for her niche. Each is a potential friend. These women might not live next door, but they do live the lifestyle and are a wonderful "virtual" resource. Many have great ideas on how to stay positive in challenging circumstances. Others have discrete tips for handling naysayers and uncouth fans. Some have solutions for just about any social, childrearing, job-juggling, or health-related situation. I adore them and count them as my own personal support system.

My advice is to seek out like-minded friends wherever they are located. The wonders of the Internet make this possible and helps everyone from everywhere cope when pettiness rears its ugly head on or off the field. It just helps so much to have friends who are in the same shoes—a group to rein you in when you want to lash back. Truly, being a coach's wife involves the art and science of tongue-biting.

Keeping Him Healthy

Since this chapter is about "*dos*" and "*don'ts*," it's worth mentioning that health is a never-ending challenge. You've probably heard this coach's wife joke: *"Any last requests before football season? Because it looks like cereal for dinner for the next 17 weeks."* Seriously, Frosted Flakes is a lot easier to serve than lasagna and salad, but we all know that culinary pressures don't just go away during the season. Just the opposite—we might even strive harder to make sure our coach-husbands have a properly cooked and nutritious dinner wrapped in cellophane or aluminum foil and waiting to be re-heated whenever he might show up for dinner.

Your man cannot exist on no sleep and fast food, although he might try it if you let him. Depending on the time of year, mine goes to work around 6, comes home around 7 to work some more, and relies on my background in nutrition to eat smart. I've sort of segued into clean eating and a vegan lifestyle, but I'm married to someone who likes a good old-fashioned barbecue sandwich. So I pack his lunches, sneak in the veggies, and encourage him to unwind with wine instead of beer.

I admit to occasionally adding a cookie or two, as well. Cookies are a staple in the world of coaching, and I'm trying to incorporate "vegan" treats into our lives. I watch "Cake Wars" with my mom, Suzanne, and love that she picked up the "art of fondant." She's so artsy, and it reminded her of polymer clay. So off she went to Walmart to buy polymer clay-looking fondant—and voila! Her cookies are a fondant-fancy hit. Someone asked if she baked fancy sugar cookies, so she began making those on the side, as well. This inspired me, of course, to step up my game in the kitchen and "invent" healthier low-fat, low-sugar versions of sweet treats.

Then there's job-related stress. The coaching profession can be strange. While one door closes for one coach, it presents an opportunity for another. Stability is sought, yet can be hard to find. Changes happen fast, the good and the bad. So I encourage Jeffrey to work out. It's good for his mind and body, and I want him in tip-top shape, so his back doesn't hurt and his feet hold up. During certain parts of the season, he wakes up super early to walk the dogs a quarter mile, and then works out for an hour or so. I usually wake up around this time and make him breakfast … although I admit, that didn't always happen toward the tail end of my pregnancy. Mommy needs her sleep too, right?

Perhaps that makes me a bit less selfless than MiMi. She made breakfast come rain, shine, or pregnancies. My mother once said, "Honestly, a lady in MiMi's day was one of these people who got up, cooked, cleaned, and made it look effortless. She managed to look beautiful doing it as well. She dressed up and put lipstick on before she ever stepped foot outside the door. And she was into real manners—a beautiful woman who was always there as an example for her children, and later her grandchildren."

So I completely understood why MiMi was horrified by my yoga pants, hair buns and lack of makeup, which was occasionally my "style" during busier-than-usual holidays and my pregnancy. However, she appreciated that I majored in nutrition science. She knew I had the educational background to attend to the nutritional needs of my little family. So I might not be an elegant chef, but I'm a great home cook and think long and hard about what appears on the dinner table.

As for mental health, Jeffrey is big on motivation and shares Zig Ziglar and Bill Parcells quotes with his student athletes. I'm always encouraging him too, sometimes to the point that he thinks I'm dropping gentle hints. "Am I doing something wrong?" he asks. "No, honey, I'm *uplifting* you," I respond. "Ahhh, okay," he says, and I remind myself that I'm dealing with a sensitive human being who gives his all, and more, to a system that demands his utmost every day.

I once overheard him say, "Erica feeds me energy, and then I feed the players energy." That's probably the biggest compliment I could ever receive. Jeffrey is the first to confirm that in his world, the perfect coach's wife is the wife that's perfect for him.

Chapter 2: Just for Us

"The characteristic that every college football coach should look for in a wife is independence."
~ Head Coach Bob Stoops

One of my favorite quotes about coaches' wives is by Head Coach Bob Stoops of the University of Oklahoma: "The characteristic that every college football coach should look for in a wife is independence." This is so incredibly accurate.

Coaching couples have to be very trusting of one another while operating independently much of the time. You hear about divorce in this profession, and I've been blessed to be around leaders in relationships and mentors in marriage. Strong women step into the role, and yes, from the home front it may feel like a selfish profession. But from the field, coaching high school football is a giving profession that changes lives. It's a calling to help kids become more than they imagined they could be.

Our roles are selfless, and that's a fact. But while our primary focus is on others—our children, husbands, and the team—it's important that wives be involved in something we are personally passionate about, as well. This could be a career, a charity, a cause, or a hobby. I once posted to my social media groups this sentiment and the "something just for us" theme: *I could not be more grateful for this life we live, and for all of the opportunities that are coming our way. New family additions, new business ventures, new travels, and new career opportunities. Even when things do not go our way, we keep the faith. We ARE making OUR DREAMS come true.*

Ellie Mallory

An excellent person to speak on this topic is Eleanor "Ellie" Mallory. She is absolutely amazing. I previously mentioned she's a founding member of the American Football Coaches' Wives

Association (AFCWA), and below I share her background of support, sisterhood, and life outside of the "football bubble."

"In 1967 or 1968 as young coach's wife located at Ohio State, I read an article written on the topic of divorce. It ranked divorces according to profession. The number one profession affected by divorce was medical, followed by the entertainment industry. Coaches' families came in next to last as far as divorce rate. The very lowest was agriculture.

I'll never forget when Coach Woody Hayes asked me, 'Why do you think this is?' Before I could commit my mouth to my brain, I said, 'We aren't together enough to get into an argument!' As my husband slipped under the table, Woody Hayes agreed. 'That's true,' he said.

Coaches' wives had many of the same issues then that they have now. Rather than social media and online news, their husbands were covered on television and newsprint. We noticed that the wives seemed to be under more stress. They did much of the childrearing themselves, and had to endure the media. Over the years, we began seeing an increase in the divorce rate stemming from these difficulties and pressures. So the women so decided to form an association at the convention.

The organization started with no money or mailing list. Without the Internet, it was an idea spread through word of mouth and phone calls. A mix of fifty high school, college and pro coaches' wives showed up at convention, and it's grown ever since. We saw a need, and that's why it has succeeded.

There are a lot of similarities with coaches' wives, political wives, and military wives as well. We're in the public view and have husbands who are very busy in their profession. You have to have a life of your own. The AFCWA was formed with this idea in mind—a tight-knit group filled with women who needed each other's company, advice, and friendship, as well as opportunities to pursue higher education and serve in their own communities."

Today, two scholarships a year are offered to assist coaches' wives in pursuing a degree. Wherever the national convention is held, the AFCWA gives a donation to a children's hospital. Dues and cookbook sales make this possible. I'm so proud to belong to this organization, where coaches' wives network, collaborate, and participate in outreach."

Susan Rodgers

Susan Rodgers is the wife of famed major college coach and Division 1 recruiting coordinator Randy Rodgers. She is the mother of Jay, Jeff, and Jonny. Susan's oldest and middle boys segued into the NFL and coach together for the Chicago Bears. Jay is a defensive line coach, and Jeff was a special teams coordinator until recently moving to the Arizona Cardinals as the Special Teams Coordinator. Not often do brothers coach on the same NFL team, but according to Susan, "It certainly made it easier for Randy and me to attend games and cheer them on!"

Susan was a teacher when she met her soon-to-be husband, who was a high school coach at the time. They began teaching again when her boys entered school. Her insights as another founding member of the AFCWA are also invaluable:

"In the coaching life, you don't live around your own family—you live where the jobs are. We landed at the University of Illinois, and then the University of Texas, so there was always some adjusting to do. But I was very happy and very proud of Randy's accomplishments. And I had a support system in other coaches' wives, especially those involved in the American Football Coach's Wife Association (AFCWA).

Decades ago, women had to find their own methods to function in the coaching world. The AFCWA helped change that. We were initially discouraged by some to join—people who felt the conventions were an "all-guys network" reserved for coaches and their XOXO talk. But we persisted, and the AFCWA grew into a networking and support group for coach's wives—a place to vent, volunteer, further support our husbands, and grow into our roles.

It eventually provided scholarships for coach's wives who dreamed of pursuing their education. Best of all, it allowed us more time with our husbands, who could occasionally take us out to dinner during conventions. The organization still exists, and many wives join."

On the Job

Lisa Mallory is the daughter-in-law of Ellie Mallory and the wife of Ellie's son Doug, the defensive backs coach for the Atlanta Falcons. Lisa recalls her mother-in-law was writing the first AFCWA newsletter when she and Doug were dating 30 years ago!

Lisa told me that when she first married Doug, she was working at a private inpatient psychiatric hospital in Western Kentucky. She didn't know many people and made friends with coworkers. This became a valuable lesson: you have to have "something" outside of football about which you are passionate. Start a book club, work at a soup kitchen, be the homeroom mom, volunteer at an animal shelter, pursue a degree, have a hobby, and cultivate friendships outside of the football circle.

"Football coaches are passionate about their jobs and work such long hours, so without something else away from it, football could swallow you," she says. "It could make wives resentful, and that would make for some miserable coaches."

For the last 15 years, Lisa has worked as a forensic interviewer for law enforcement. She's done more than a thousand interviews in five different states. Prior to that, she was a child and family therapist. It's a job that matters, and her husband is proud of her. "You can't just be the cheerleader all the time, and sometimes that role is reversed. My husband is my biggest cheerleader and supporter, and I think that my career alleviates his feelings of guilt since he's gone so much. He knows I'm busy and fulfilled," she says. And although she's deeply connected to football and other coaches' wives, this is her life outside of football—her "something just for her."

***

Julie West is an inspirational coach's wife and art teacher at the Brenham High School. Her husband Glenn is the Athletic Director and Head Football Coach, and came onboard after my grandfather, Lloyd Wassermann, left Brenham for Nederland. Julie has been like a mother to other coach's wives and many of the football players. Previous to teaching, she earned a degree in advertising and had an illustrious career at Ogilvy & Mather, Lyric Studios, and other companies where she served as art director. She even worked on the children's television show, Barney!

Like her own mother, she segued into teaching and has a passion for helping dyslexic students. Her own girls were diagnosed with dyslexia in elementary school and are now advocates, themselves. Julie notes that many coaches' wives choose careers that are more flexible and easily relocatable, such graphic design, healthcare, IT, and teaching. She also mentioned that her daughters are dating coaches! More on that later!

***

Some coaches' wives, even back in the '60s and '70s, worked outside the home. Lois Faigle was a close friend of my grandmother and a substitute teacher for one year, which was a part-time job that worked beautifully with her children's schedules. My grandmother occasionally babysat for her while she worked. "It helped that the high school kids knew that I was coach Faigle's wife," says Lois. "I also finished my bachelor's degree and taught there for two years."

MiMi was a substitute teacher as well while her children were in school, and PaPa told me that she introduced herself to the class by writing "Mrs. Wassermann" on the blackboard. The kids would say, "Uh oh, are you the coach's wife?" The students were held to high standards, with both academic and athletic policy books handed out at the beginning of the year. But they appeared to be even more well-behaved in "Mrs. Wassermann's" class, and she never had any trouble teaching PaPa's athletes.

MiMi also told me that coaches earned next to nothing in those early days. PaPa remembers a time in his career when he was paid $300 a month as a coach, and MiMi made more money working as a secretary for the school district early in the first years of their marriage! Yes, she and many others managed to wear both hats—coach's wife and working girl—and maintained her sweet disposition.

***

Ellie Mallory shared that she was a music major who knew nothing about athletics "Absolutely nothing I had no idea how football was played when Bill and I were engaged. He took me to a football game and didn't want to explain the game—he wanted to watch the game.

'Just look at the scoreboard,' he said.

'The scoreboard says down two, so the scoreboard is wrong,' she said.

Bill, puzzled, looked at her, and she explained, 'There are eight guys down.'

The family still jokes about this, but the Ellie + Bill combination has worked out splendidly. Ellie finished her master's degree and became an elementary school music teacher as Bill became a head coach. Ellie learned the game of football, but also learned how to mentor other coaches' wives as they entered the culture. Showing new wives "the ropes" is something every seasoned coach's wife can do!

***

My friend Lisa Gotte, married to Athletic Coordinator BJ Gotte of Paetow High School, has a career in property management. Jordan Harrell, wife of Coach Clark Harrell, has a popular blog. I have a job in sports journalism. So many of us have professions outside of our duties as coaches' wives, and this may be out of necessity or choice. Regardless, it offers "just for us" time and provides respite from the football field, if only briefly. The consensus seems to be that this is healthy and fulfilling, but also turns us into "multi-tasking mamas" which I address later in the book.

***

Each year the High School Coaches Wives Association (THSCWA) honors a very special coach's wife who has gone above and beyond obstacles or simply let her light shine brighter for others. The 2017 recipient of the Wife of the Year award is Rhonda Clayton, wife of Cinco Ranch Head Coach Don Clayton. Rhonda knew Mimi, and her husband worked under Papa, so I was thrilled that she was chosen.

Over the course of her marriage, she and Don relocated five times, but it all started in Nederland. Rhonda told me, "Your grandmother was a wonderful role model in my first year. Don and I were engaged at the time, and she and the other wives in Nederland included me in everything." During her 34-year career as a teacher, while raising daughters Lindsay and Lacey, she attended every game—and still does. As the daughter of a coach herself, she knows how important it is to be in the bleachers, supporting her husband and the players, even while handling the responsibilities of a classroom and young students.

Chapter 3: Time is Treasure

Time is not measured by clocks, but by moments."
~ **Anonymous**

Time is a commodity in a coach's household. The smallest act of togetherness is a big deal since even small interactions can be few and far between during football season. There are a lot of nice things we do for our husbands morning, noon, and night, just because. But we do much more than nice things because we have to. It's our primary responsibility. Time and dedication are major factors, as all coaches' wives can attest.

Thank heavens I knew what I was getting into when I married Jeffrey Barnett. And vice versa. Honestly, if a coach is going to get married, his prospective wife has probably already been tried and tested through a season or two. She understands the ginormous time commitment coaching requires. It's not for the faint of heart. It's not for the clingy, insecure or needy. A quote from Coach Joe Gibbs underscores what is often the stark reality: "This isn't an easy lifestyle for a coach's wife. The coach is the guy who stands up and hears everyone tell him how great he is. The wife is the one waiting at home alone while the coach is spending every night at the office."

This notion takes me back to the details of the first football game I ever attended. It was at one of PaPa's Texas A&M Consolidated games, and I had just started elementary school. I was watching football on TV at an even a younger age, so sports became ingrained. I remember how much I loved wearing A&M volleyball and football shirts. I remember playing t-ball. So as you can imagine, being raised in a family of coaches and athletes made it "natural" for me to date sports guys.

I met Jeffrey in Dallas as I was working a game. I came up to the press box and made a comment about a play, and he overheard. I think he was shocked that I knew exactly what was going on and wasn't afraid to express my opinion. We met back up and went bar hopping to find a football game we wanted to watch. I remember him saying, "You are a pretty intense chick," which I took as a compliment.

"What are we doing Saturday?" he asked.

"Watching football," I answered.

"What are we doing Sunday?" he asked.

"Watching football," I answered, letting him know that NFL is one of my many niches. I love that it's something we can spend time doing together and enjoying together.

Finding Time

I love the saying that *Time is not measured by clocks, but by moments.* Sometimes our husbands find little ways to make those moments happen. For instance, Susan Rodgers once told me that her often-absent husband folded towels for her every morning (when he was home) before he left for work—just because. What a sweet gesture! It was his way of contributing a small act of devotion, which meant the world to Susan. It was thoughtful and saved her time. I bet that after reading this, some wives will probably be nudging their husbands in the ribs and pointing to this part of the book, as in, *hint, hint.*

I can't tell you how many newspaper clippings MiMi saved to prepare me to become a coach's wife. Inevitably, "finding time" was an ongoing challenge back then, and still is today. I remember when Jeffrey got wrapped up in a football game and got home close to 3 a.m. But he was still up early to install our first car seat. Exhausting, I know, but sweet baby Noah was due in a month, and Jeffrey did what he had to do … and didn't think twice about it. That might sound like a little moment, but to me it was huge!

I once moved us into a new house right at the end of summer while Jeffrey was off in Thibodaux doing the annual Manning

Passing Academy Camp, and then flew to Dallas and Nebraska. He never saw the house until he arrived back in Texas. After hearing this story, a non-sports friend (who is a fellow journalist) couldn't contain herself. She shot off questions in quick succession: What is the hardest part about being a coach-husband? Is it the juggling? Do you worry about being away for extended amounts of time? Do you miss the home front? Do you worry about nurturing the relationship when you are pulled in so many directions … and how do you address that?

My husband, bless his heart, answered: "Yes, the juggling is hard. Yes, I worry about traveling. Yes, I miss the home front. Yes, I worry about my relationship. I was a bachelor and committed to coaching for the long haul, so I knew the uphill battle I had in store finding someone who understood the 'coach life,' as Erica puts it. But she basically green lights my success. She handles "life" while I take care of the team. The coach's wife matters more than any coaching husband can really describe."

Date Night

Coach's wife Lisa Gotte once mentioned the importance of "date night." I must admit, I now look at date nights differently—they are that important. She told me, "Date nights are hard during football season, but you need dates nights, and you have to make it happen. Even if it means scouting games with your husband, the point is to be together and spend some time alone. That's where you communicate. That's when you tell him what you need, and vice versa. If I need more time with him, I tell him, and he makes time. I don't know how he does it, but he finds the time. And vice versa. You can't be a good wife if you can't find that balance, so make time for it."

Lisa also gives this advice to new wives: "I'm a secure person, and I can see that women who have to be around their significant others all the time might struggle. The biggest thing is that you have to be patient and supportive. Your husband is going to spend a lot of time at the field house and a lot of time with other people.

You have to make sure you spend time together too, and this might mean going to the banquets, the games, the field house, and the practices."

I love this advice, and believe me, Jeffrey and I are focusing on stepping up our date nights. Stealing time together at home is one thing, but I'd like to make it a more formal recurring event in our lives—something that is scheduled and on our calendars. I agree with Lisa that it's a worthwhile and necessary investment in a marriage.

The Season

So there's "the season," "the holidays," and "the off-season." Nowadays, it seems that each requires the same amount of effort from my coach-husband, who leaves early to be with his players and may arrive home at 7 p.m., 8 p.m., 10 p.m. or midnight. In August, a sense of excitement is in the air. And for coaches wives, it signals "See you in the spring!"—but even that's a fallacy. You'll see why I think so later in the chapter.

The season starts with fall camp and practices, which take place in the summer. In the case of Texas, that might mean a blazing hot, 100-degree summer. Soon the players are in their first day of full pads, despite the temperature. What and how players eat, drink, and sleep matters mightily, for fall camp separates the starters from the rest.

On top of this, coaches grade film, evaluate players, and handle upcoming freshmen who haven't been involved in the program and have to be taught everything. Their parents have to be taught too, from the football culture to "what to expect." It's a huge challenge, and sometimes Jeffrey picks up kids in the morning to make sure they get to workouts if they aren't able to drive or their parents can't make it. Some parents don't understand that the kids must be there.

Then fall camp ends, scrimmages begin, school starts, and the first game has everyone pumped. It's an all-consuming time of the year.

For instance, I just love it when my husband winks and tells me at the beginning of the week, "See you on Saturday, love!" My absolute favorite is: "See you after playoffs!"

The Friday night games do lead to the playoffs, but first, we have to get through October. This is a month when a heck of a lot of wives are just completely done. I call it the first "holiday month" because it's an important occasion for our kids, who may or may not get to carve pumpkins or trick-or-treat with their fathers on Halloween. Then here come the playoffs, wreaking havoc and chaos because there's always some sort of personal scheduling conflict hinging on a win or loss.

Of course, we want our coaches to win and take their team as far as they can, but again, we also might (secretly) just want football season to end. It's an ambivalent feeling, a tug-of-war of emotions, and I'm just being honest. After all, the hardcore holidays are just ahead. In the world outside of coaching, these special occasions are spent with family and friends. But if you are playing football leading up to Thanksgiving, you have to explain to relatives (who may not understand) that you might not be there on Turkey Day. This can, and has, divided families and caused rifts.

Or you might travel to be with loved ones and leave your coach behind, because he wants it that way. He doesn't want to prevent you or your children from seeing grandparents, aunts, uncles, and cousins. And then everyone misses him terribly, which can put a damper on the occasion. But in this lifestyle, perseverance is key and we motor on, adapting as best we can and teaching joy, thankfulness, flexibility and adaptability to our kiddos in the process.

The Big Holidays

We can't really plan anything during the major holidays, especially in Texas, where playoffs occur in November or December and last longer than anywhere else in the nation. So when I was pregnant with my "playoff baby" I wasn't sure where Jeffrey would be when our son was born! By the way, Noah was due on December 2nd and arrived December 8th. I'm pretty sure this will be the last time he's "late" for anything for the rest of his life, considering the family he's been born into.

Again, our lives hang on each win or a loss, and worse, our husbands might be super sad during Thanksgiving because the team was defeated. They may be coping with that emotionally well into the new year, and this means your coach may not to be "present" even if he is sitting in the same room. Your own emotions will have to be put on hold as you help him adjust.

This can be hard on a marriage and is why communication is so huge, especially leading into the Christmas season. But how do we communicate when we are so busy? Well, I try to stay organized and write down my hopes, desires, and dreams for Christmas and New Year's Eve. I plan shopping trips, decorations, and expeditions to see the Christmas lights. We can hope to do a little caroling in the neighborhood and spread good cheer … but that's often a pipe dream. Whenever possible, these little occasions become opportunities to talk. When I have alone time with my husband—especially when doing something seasonal and locked in a car together—there is time to communicate.

Of course, I then wonder how these special occasions will actually pan out. Paige Thurmond, daughter of collegiate coaching great Chris Thurmond, has an interesting observation on holidays. She thinks there should be "Christmas in July" for coaching families, because the holidays are full of question marks, especially for kids: Who will be fired? Will we have to move? Will another coach's kid (and best friend) move away? July seems to be a more serene month, with jobs nailed down and fall camp on the horizon. More of Paige's insights, plus contributions from other kids, appear in the "Coaches' Kids" chapter.

Basically, you just do your best juggling act until January 1st. If your team plays in the state championship, you might have a bit longer to wait, of course. But the payoff to enduring such a grueling stretch of months is supposed to be the off-season.

The Off-Season

Coach's wife and blogger Jordan Harrell once told me, "The hardest part about being a coach's wife to me are the transitions between seasons. With each transition comes different expectations, and sometimes they aren't spoken out loud which complicates things even more. During the season, I expect to have to do everything, but appreciate his help when he offers it. My love language is acts of service, so when he's really busy I feel neglected because he doesn't have time to help me. I have learned (or am learning) to not take it personally and communicate better."

She adds, "During off-season, I expect to NOT do everything. And those changing roles are hard to navigate. Who is now responsible for what? There's usually a week or two readjusting period where the waters feel a little choppy, but they smooth out once we get into a routine."

***

My take on the off-season is… *what's the off-season? It's a myth, that's what it is.* There are never really any breaks, and it may actually be crunch time during January and February as your coach travels to clinics and also focuses on helping student athletes with private drills, voluntary workouts, and a conditioning program. There is always someone who needs help in the weight room or on the field with size, strength, speed, power, and balance. And coaches never stop mentally reviewing the prior season and assessing performance and (they can't help themselves): one-on-one drills, passing, catching, interceptions, sacks, and shutouts.

At the end of March and the beginning of April, there's spring ball. Now some school districts, like Dallas, have spring ball. Others, like Houston, don't because it's always raining and flooding. Houston is just 35 feet above sea level and flat as a tabletop. We get 50 inches a year and occasional severe thunderstorms, or even hurricanes, that raise those inches significantly in a matter of days. So spring ball depends on where you are located, how the program is run, and how a school district chooses to use its TTL hours

Multi-tasking Mamas

Pro-level coaches' wives might travel by plane. Collegiate coaches' wives might do the same but can also travel on buses for one or two away games. In high school, coaches' wives have to drive. So I drive. Jeffrey looks for me in stands, sometimes with binoculars, and checks in with me from the field. I give him a little nod and wave, and it helps him to keep battling through turnovers or giving up sacks. It makes scoring a touch down that much sweeter because we share that together and I can talk about the body of work he created during the game.

In addition to my own career, I clean the house, care for the baby, cook meals, check the mail, pay the bills, schedule my husband's dentist appointments, ask about his day, and let him talk. He needs to get his emotions out. He needs to vent, which usually sounds something like this: *This kid didn't have a good practice, the team looks great on film, I'm not sure if we can pick up the blitz, I have 12 missed text messages from last night from all over the country …*

This is not slavish devotion. I'm not a Stepford wife, and neither was my MiMi. What she was, and what I am, is a partner to a coach in an unconventional marriage. If you think about it, and as Ellie Mallory mentioned to me, the two hardest jobs are being a military wife and a coach's wife … well, perhaps an ER doctor's wife belongs in this category too. Absence is the norm, and those special stretches of bonding time are few and far between.

The ability to multi-task truly matters. Sometimes I get a text: "Hey honey, I forgot my lunch!" If I'm not traveling, I can hustle his lunch to campus and enjoy spending a few precious minutes with him. He won't admit to this, but sometimes I suspect he "forgets" on purpose just to steal extra face time with me! So it's the little moments that count, like the time we share at our only family dinner during football season—on Sundays—and even that gets iffy. If we are lucky, we might be able to sneak in a rare movie night (if he isn't watching film)!

I'm also always looking for timesavers—ways to work smarter, not harder. Life hacks, tricks, and shortcuts are now my "thing," and there's actually a lifehack.org website with a gazillion ideas for easier living. You can try boredpanda.com/life-hacks/ too. Today I pay bills online or set up auto pay. Amazon Prime has become the greatest thing ever because it saves money and the shipping is free. When I was pregnant, working, and traveling all at the same time, I began ordering groceries online and had them delivered via Instacart. It cost a bit more, but was worth it (because otherwise it might not get done, which would stress me out).

The bottom line is, my heart belongs to a coach. Taking care of him brings me joy, and it's easier when I'm super organized. That's my job amidst many other jobs in our very busy lives.

Family Planning

Some coaching couples actually plan pregnancies to accommodate the football season. Oh yes, they certainly do! But what about weddings?

Jeffrey and I planned our wedding around the weekend of the Lone Star Coaching Clinic in Bryan/College station while I was traveling and he was coaching. It was the playoffs, and the timing was crazy, but still perfect. We rented the Brazos Cotton Exchange and loved that our names and the wedding event appeared on the marquee at the Palace Theater and the Queen Theater, while our guests stayed at the historic La Salle Hotel. It complemented our vintage winter wonderland theme.

The venue and ceremony was a lot of fun and very practical, since so many of our guests were coaches attending the clinic. We had downtown Bryan to ourselves, and (at least from my perspective) the whole thing went off without a hitch—or perhaps I should say it went off *with* a hitch, because Jeffrey and I certainly did get hitched. My mother was my wedding planner and designed the décor, the cake, and the whole 9 yards. The memories are still fresh and exciting in my mind, but I must say I'm particularly proud that we were able to coordinate a lovely event and simultaneously accommodate the schedules of our guests.

My Season

One of my more recent blog posts was a year-end wrap up of 2017. Normally these retrospectives have everything to do with football, but this time I shared my "season" through the lens of trimesters. So much occurred during conception, pregnancy, and birth that it had my head spinning. I'm sharing this "season" below:

Greetings! With the holidays approaching, it's once again time to write a year-end post. Normally this would include a recap of a great and glorious football season. But this year, 2017, I had my own 'season' which happened to be broken into trimesters.

So here's a snapshot of what that journey looked like, and the highs and lows that I'm recollecting after giving birth to my first born, Noah, on December 8th.

First trimester: I found out I was pregnant while dealing with a torn meniscus. During this time, my grandmother, Betty Wassermann, was struggling with severe health issues. I can't begin to describe what MiMi meant to me. She was a coaches' wife before there were a lot of resources for coaches' wives, and pioneered the sisterhood for us all. Thanks to her, I was well prepared to marry into the culture. I know my coach-husband, Jeffrey, appreciates that!

We weren't going to announce the pregnancy due to three miscarriages and the fear I might not be able to carry a baby to term. But MiMi, despite a strong battle with heart issues and other medical problems, was slipping a bit. She now faced a leg amputation, but kept insisting, "I'm going to get better." Still, her health was steadily declining. My PaPa, Lloyd Wassermann, said to me privately, "You have to tell her about the baby. You have to. It will give her hope."

So at 13 weeks, after an appointment for gender testing, we were able to tell MiMi that I had conceived and was carrying a boy. We even had the name picked out—Noah—and she was the first to hear it! The news was a huge pick-me-up. It had MiMi going from zero to 100! She kept saying, "I need to be strong so I can be here for the baby!" Everyone, and I mean everyone, thought she would be okay and pull through, and I felt so much hope, joy, and frankly, pressure, as I carried Noah. So much hinged on this pregnancy.

Second Trimester: MiMi went through the amputation and was fine. And then we lost her at the end of May I entered my second trimester. It was such a shock because we really thought she would live for another decade, at least. I can't begin to describe the grief, and not just my own. The whole coaching community and every life she touched reeled at the news. It was then that I knew I'd write a book in her honor—a book that covered the fifty-year arc of her life as a coach's wife, mother, and grandmother. Now we would face a series of firsts ... first 4th of July, birthday, anniversary and upcoming holidays without her. I'm still adjusting to this "new normal."

Jeffrey was gone a lot for work. Luckily, I was able to attend two camps with him because I was working those camps. That's the beauty of what I do. And I had to coordinate a move by myself due to his new position, and began scouting houses that suited us and making sure our new home was located near a park so that I could walk and have a place to play with the baby once he arrived.

I chose our new home by myself as Jeffrey traveled extensively out of state. And I moved us in, lock, stock, and barrel, sort of like a single pregnant person. If you are a coach's wife, you know what I mean. Then I began decorating, all the while taking sports journalism assignments and writing a book. Thank heavens my mom came to help, and thank heavens Jeffrey loved our new home. Honestly, I like living out in the middle of nowhere, so living in this neighborhood was a new experience—one I've grown to appreciate. I was now closer to stores and amenities and family-friendly doctors offices, so that was a good thing.

Our old house had been affected by the 50-year flooding in the Brazos River area and was still under renovation. Had we stayed there, we would have been under water. Friends sent us pictures, and our reaction was, "Whew! We dodged a bullet!" It felt like a miracle that the hurricane left our new house untouched. Our area in Cinco Ranch didn't flood at all. The lights flickered only once. We could hear the evacuation helicopters flying overhead all around us, and we prayed for the people in Katy and Richmond who lost everything. It was heartbreaking. We kept saying we were safe because of Noah (our yet-to-be-born baby)—like Noah's Ark. What a blessing that our neighbors had built our house. They told us they chose this area because the future irrigation plans meant we would not flood.

It was Jeffrey's last season as a JV coach—his last year before the crazy Friday and Saturday night games. His teaching schedule remained crazy, and he worked 5:30 a.m. until 8:00 p.m. continuously. This meant he could only attend one obstetric appointment, and that had been the gender appointment before MiMi passed away. My first baby shower, hosted by dear friend and baseball great Bo Porter and his wife Stacy, was postponed until after the hurricane passed. Stacy, bless her, rescheduled it at the end of August, and opening the gifts made the notion of motherhood so very real!

Third Trimester: I had a birthday, and Jeffrey surprised me with a new car! I enjoyed a second baby shower, hosted by a wonderful coach's family down the street. Bless them, for the celebration was exciting and introduced me to new friends. That's what's so special about our coaching culture. Wives are embraced and welcomed and supported by strangers who quickly become family. I don't know of another profession that does this. It's amazing to experience first hand as a newbie to the area.

From September to December Jeffrey focused on the program for a brand new school. He was developing and planning the launch of a new football app at the same time. I prepped for the baby, relaunched my website, and continued writing the book. The playoff season approached, and I began counting down the weeks, and then days, until Noah was born. December 2nd could not arrive quickly enough! I was so excited at the thought of being a new mom.

December 2nd came and went. I thought, *Okay, I'll just keep working from home. What are the hundred things I can accomplish today?* In fact, I worked while in labor. Yes, I walked and walked and used my smart phone to blog, collaborate with my book editor, coordinate the book cover with my graphic designer, beta test Jeffrey's app, and more, in between contractions. Jeffrey thought I was nuts when I told him to sleep while I walked some more.

"But you're in labor," he protested.

"And you're exhausted," I said. "I can use this time to get some things off my plate."

Fourth Trimester: I'm writing about a "fourth trimester" because recovering from childbirth and adapting to motherhood is a season in itself. At last, on December 8th, our post-40 week bundle of joy arrived at 2:48 a.m. in the midst of unusual seasonal weather. It was snowing during his birth—an odd occurrence in the Houston area. In fact, Channel 2 ran a piece explaining just how rare snow is in our neck of the woods, stating, "Going back two decades, there have been only five snowfall events in Houston, and only three of those measured more than a trace." And since a whopping 0.7 inches of snow fell at George Bush Intercontinental Airport, the official reporting station for the city of Houston, we now have a memorable birthing story to share with Noah some day. According to the statistics, he'll probably be in first grade by the time it snows again in our neighborhood!

Noah was a beautiful newborn. I'm not just saying that because I'm his mother. He really was beautiful right out of the womb! I was what the doctors called "post hemorrhage" because they had to clean out scar tissue before Noah could be born. I had a torn labia that required stitches. They kept us in the hospital for four days, just to be sure.

It has been a lot of fun texting photos of Noah to family and friends, and he's so cute in his "Noah's Ark" nursery. My little guy is eating his fingers, toes, breast milk and formula. Between breastfeeding, diaper changes, and a baby who hasn't yet developed a schedule, I'm super busy. It's a different kind of busy because I'm balancing feelings of exhaustion and emotion and hormones and a strong maternal protectiveness.

So I rest while he sleeps, except when I'm working. For example, at two weeks old, Noah joined Jeffrey, me, and my mother-in-law at the Texas High School State Championships. I must say that I was nervous traveling with such a tiny infant, but he was a trooper. Thankfully, the hard work prior to, during, and after his birth paid off, which means my projects are in good shape and our future going into the new year looks wonderful and promising and exciting.

So as my personal "season" winds down, I send prayers, well wishes, joy, and happiness to the coalition of fellow coach's wives as we continue to celebrate our unique roles in the sports world.

Chapter 4: Family, Faith, and Football

"Coaches hold a special place in the lives of our young people ... and behind that coach is often a wife making his career possible."
~ Fellowship of Christian Athletes Greenville

Nowadays, it may seem like we have to tiptoe around our beliefs based on recent developments in the news. Coaches have been punished for living their faith on the field, and a few examples follow. Back in 2014, Melissa Brittain, wife of Tempe Prep football coach Tommy Brittain, confirmed online that her husband was suspended two weeks for praying with his team. This past summer, former Bremerton High assistant coach Joe Kennedy was punished for silently praying on one knee midfield after football games, and the U.S. 9th Circuit Court of Appeals said his religious liberties did not apply and were not protected. Just this fall, East Coweta High School Coach John Small was not allowed to bow his head in prayer with his players.

This is such a stark contrast to the tradition of praying in the locker room, on the field, and with the players. It brings to mind the glory days my PaPa experienced in his illustrious coaching career. Some might call PaPa an "old school" type of coach who openly practices an "old school" type of faith. This is a man who was inducted into the Brenham High School Hall of Honor and coached one or two All Americans among other professional players. In fact, he put seven players into the NFL. PaPa retired after 44 years and has seen it all—lots of changes in the game and society as a whole. He said, "From a Christian standpoint, I didn't allow players or my coaches to do crazy things or curse on the field. We had after-game parties and rotated from one coaches' home to another. I strived to do this every place I coached, and was proud that Betty represented our family so well."

When he coached at Nederland, he and the players kneeled in the locker room and said a prayer before the game. After the game, players either congratulated each other or consoled each other, and then kneeled and said the Lord's Prayer. There was not one football player who didn't participate, and this was typical in many Texas towns. Today, however, it's almost unheard of today.

Once, decades ago, while kneeling on 50-yard line, PaPa noticed two women he didn't know coming across the field. Suddenly something hit him in the head—one of the women took her purse and whacked him. He was dazed and almost knocked unconscious, and the assistant coaches came running. Of course, PaPa wanted to find out why he was assaulted. Was it because of the praying? Was it because of the team's performance? Of course, today there would almost certainly be an arrest. But back then, things were different. Although PaPa was tempted to file charges, the school superintendent said, "Why would you say that? The person who hit you was the mother of the quarterback and the wife a higher up." So PaPa left the whole matter alone (although MiMi was outraged, of course), but will hopefully write a book about these types of escapades and many other adventures he experienced as a head coach.

This story brings to mind the importance of faith in the lives of coaches families, even when that faith is challenged.

Ministry

I believe MiMi's personal support system came almost entirely from her faith, and she certainly encouraged me to join the Fellowship of Christian Athletes Coaches' Wives Ministry. I assume from this encouragement that she was also a member, although I never asked specifically. I do know that the Fellowship of Christian Athletes (FCA) is a wonderful interdenominational Christian sports ministry founded in 1954 "to see the world impacted for Jesus Christ through the influence of coaches and athletes." MiMi was so pleased with the FCA Coaches' Wives

Ministry mantra: *"The coach is the heart of the game. The wife is the heartbeat."*

I encourage other coaches' wives to check out the FCA Coaches' Wives Ministry at fcacwm.org and join! I love their "Who We Are" page, which states, "Since 1954, the Lord has been impacting lives across the nation and internationally through FCA. Our philosophy is to minister "to and through the coach." And the "4 C's" of FCA are coaches, camps, community, and campuses. Camps are opportunities for impact, the community and campuses are the places of influence. In the middle of it all is the coach— and his wife."

Another great ministry is The Reach—A Ministry for Coaches' Wives that intentionally connects wives with each other. It filters everyday life through the word of God and inspires healthy, meaningful discussions concerning the challenges of the lifestyle. It's a part of coachesoutreach.org and includes 400 wives meeting all over the state of Texas, with groups in Alabama, Mississippi, and Oklahoma as well. There are requests to join in Florida, Georgia, Kansas, Missouri, New Mexico, and Tennessee.

The coaches' wives meetings are formed geographically, and each small group coordinates their own meeting times and locations based on the schedules of their group members. Genuine friendships bloom based on commonality, trust, and the truth of God's Word. Please check it out if you are interested in another source of Christian support.

Chase Relationships, Not Titles

Indeed, it really does feel at times that the coaching life has roots in ministry. I'm reminded of this by Jordan Harrell, a former 6th grade math teacher and coach. The last five years she's been a stay-at-home-mom to her three kids, the oldest of whom just started kindergarten. She loves chocolate, naps, coffee, her family, and cute shoes, not necessarily in that order. But also maybe in that order. She is now a freelance writer and blogger at

Jordanharrell.com and fridaynightwives.com—and her insights are great!

"Clark and I both feel as though his job is our ministry, that coaching is as 'boots on the ground' as being a missionary or a preacher. He is forming relationships with kids who need him, and need Jesus. And my job is to help facilitate that. We have the kids over for dinner. He stays after practice sometimes and talks to a hurting kid, which makes him even later, but I have to constantly remind myself what my purpose is. We are seeking his kingdom first, and expecting 'all these things to be added unto us.'

The biggest lesson we have learned is to not chase titles. Chase relationships. You are happier when you are working with people you love in a positive, enjoyable atmosphere. If going to work is stressful, it won't matter how much money you are making or how high on the totem pole you are, you are going to be miserable. Go where you know you will enjoy going to work, not the place that will make you the most money or is the fastest way to get to a head coaching position. And the kids can tell – when the coaching staff enjoys each other and there's not any dissension, they feed off of that.

Being a coach's wife is hard. But so are a lot of jobs. I don't think we've cornered the market on challenging marriages but I think the enemy will try to convince us that we have – he will encourage our pity parties and remind us how often our husbands are gone. It's so important to focus on the positive, not to the extent that we hide the issues, but to the extent that we don't drown in a sea of negativity.

I spend most of my days picking up toys, wiping bottoms, and teaching small humans basic social skills. My kids, now 5, 4, and 2, are finally getting self-sufficient enough that I can get things done even when they are awake, which makes a huge difference. Writing keeps me grounded and connected to people during a stressful and often lonely time, so that's my "me time" during nap time and bedtime. My hope is that I always offer relief to others – whether that be by reminding them of the message of the cross, or telling honest stories of how I'm currently failing miserably at life, or reassuring them that they are not alone – I passionately want to spread good news, not add to others' anxiety by making them feel like they aren't measuring up."

Wives and Prayer

Once LSU football coach Ed Orgeron (married to Kelly Orgeron) was asked if he had a "coach." I love his answer: "No question. Number one, my wife ... and number two, Pastor Jacob and Pastor Steve."

Claudette Giles-Gillespie, wife of Valdosta High School head football coach Rance Gillespie, encourages people to look closely at two scriptures she holds dear: Colossians 3:23—*Whatever you do, do your work heartily, as for the Lord rather than for men,* and Micah 6:8—*He has told you, O man, what is good; And what does the Lord require of you but to do justice, to love kindness, and to walk humbly with your God.* I love that she says, "This is an awesome challenge we all have regardless of the lives or careers we have. Celebrating life with wins is always the goal of a coach, the prayer of his wife, and of course the hope or expectation of others."

It's definitely worth noting that coaches' wives stand in the gap for many, not just through physical acts of hugs and baking and encouraging words, but through prayer. Examples of prayers are all around us. Oakland Raiders Derek Carr and his wife Heather prayed unceasingly when their son, Dallas, was born with intestinal issues and underwent multiple surgeries. "We had so many people praying for us," Heather said. "The whole community came together and prayed for us. It's just amazing how many people come together in a time of need." Thankfully, Dallas recovered and was joined in 2016 by little brother Deker.

When Wendy Anderson, the wife of Arkansas State head football coach Blake Anderson, battled breast cancer, the team honored with a pink banner that stated: "Get well soon Wendy Anderson." The assistant head coach, Trooper Taylor, asked Arkansas State fans to pray for her. Blake Anderson tweeted thanks to all who prayed for his wife ,and later tweeted that Wendy was cancer-free.

Coach's wife Janice Archer, a dear friend of my grandparents Betty and Lloyd, had a special connection with my grandmother. MiMi was a very devoted Catholic, and at that time Janice had become a new Christian and member of the Methodist church. "I shared some of my faith with Betty, and when Betty's father died I told her, 'I'm going to pray with you.' We actually went into the laundry room at Betty's house, where we wouldn't be disturbed. She commented over the years that she never forgot I went out to her house to pray with her. Whenever something happened, she always called to ask if we could pray together."

When my uncle Mark Wassermann got cancer, MiMi called Janice and asked that she put her son on the prayer list at church. Janice reminded me that when one of the football players broke his neck or back and was paralyzed, MiMi and PaPa rallied the community, and raised funds to purchase a van with an automatic lift. "That's the type of Christians they were," says Janice.

***

My friend Lisa Gotte told me that "God is first and the marriage is second." Therefore, she and her husband BJ make sure church is a priority. "If he has to work on Sunday, we go to an earlier service or a Saturday night service," she says. This is a great no-excuse example for Jeffrey and me, and I'm sure many other coaching couples. I love Lakewood Church in Houston, and with Noah being so tiny, it's wonderful that I can watch Joel Osteen's worship services over the computer.

***

I also really love the writing of Carolyn Allen, especially her "Prayer for the Coach's Wife"—a lovely poem that has gone viral.

Dear Lord,

I am a coach's wife who needs You.
All I have comes from heaven; therefore,
I praise You for my teammate and his calling to be a coach,
my circumstances of daily victories and defeats,
and my faith to get me through.

You are not surprised that I feel overwhelmed during the season.
Be near me and give me strength and peace.
Help me to love others and bear fruit by
filling me with your Presence.

May I courageously run the race you have set before me,
focusing on Jesus Christ, the Author and Perfecter of my faith.

In Your Name I pray.
Amen.

Give Me Strength!

More t-shirt sightings! I spotted a wife wearing a tee that said
"Shhhh…it's the coach's old lady." This exemplifies precisely how
I feel when the slings and arrows are flying after a loss or after a
shakeup. *Shhhh! I don't want to hear it! I don't want my son to hear it!*

I love the way Lisa Nu'u articulates her faith and also shares
insights that can give us strength when our coaches (and by
association, our families) are under attack. She's the wife of
linebackers coach Joe Nu'u of Valor Christian High School and
wrote an open letter—a "Thank You Letter"—to coaches' wives
that deserves a shout out, especially because it addresses
something I struggle with. I have mentioned before, and I'll say
again, that it is an ongoing challenge for me to gracefully deal with
unjust or overly harsh criticism, and Lisa's words resonate:

> "There are times when you're at the game and you hear
> people criticizing your husband or calling him names that
> you would never dream of calling anyone else. You now

45

have to move because you don't want your kids to hear the horrible things being said about their father. You do all this because you know that God has a plan for you and your husband in the lives of the athletes He has given you to love and care for. Most of the time, it seems the athletes, parents and fans don't see all you have to sacrifice, but I want you to know that God sees your sacrifice. He sees all that you do behind the scenes so that your husband can fulfill his call as a coach, knowing that you're with him, no matter what. And I believe He is smiling down on you."

The Jewish Faith

Although it seems that many coaching families share Christian beliefs within various denominations, there are wonderful organizations for coaches of the Jewish faith. For instance, Jewish Coaches Association (JCA) is a 501c3 non-profit with the primary purpose of fostering the growth and development of individuals of the Jewish faith at all levels of sports, both nationally and internationally. The JCA is committed to creating a constructive and tolerant environment and presents the Red Auerbach Award, given annually to the nation's top Jewish college coach, as voted on by the members of the JCA. They recently announced four finalists for the 2017 Red Auerbach College Coach of the Year Award.

The American Jewish Coaches Association, located in Austin, Texas, addresses significant issues pertaining to the participation and employment of individuals of the Jewish faith in sports in general, and intercollegiate athletics in particular. It provides professional and leadership development strategies for member coaches and networking opportunities for Jewish coaches and athletic administrators. It also inspires members to coach with integrity and Jewish values and serve as a role model to their teams and communities.

Chapter 5: Teamwork

"I appreciate my wife, Beth, so much. We've always done things as a team, not just me going my own way. That's essential if you want your marriage to work."
~ Coach Lou Holtz

Once I traveled on assignment to cover a college game and remember seeing a woman wearing a t-shirt that said: MRS. COACH. I thought the big, bold lettering was hilarious and a bit daring. Coaches' wives don't usually broadcast their "title" for fear of 1.) being braggy, 2.) stealing the limelight from their husbands, or 3.) getting pelted with a banana after a high-stakes loss.

But the truth is, we are precisely that—"Mrs. Coach"—because our husband's title has everything to do with how we live, love, and raise families. "Yes, I'm with the coach," and "I'm married to football," and "I'm married to the game," and "We interrupt this marriage for football season" are all common threads in the tapestry of being the "other half." Most coaches would call us the "better half." We and our husbands are a team, are we not?

Teamwork Defined

If you look up the definition of the word "teamwork," it's described as:

> *Cooperative or coordinated effort on the part of a group of persons acting together as a team or in the interests of a common cause.*

The late, great NFL coach Vince Lombardi defined it as:

> *Individual commitment to a group effort — that is what makes a team work, a company work, a society work, a civilization work*

But my PaPa really nailed the definition when he said:

"The reason Betty and I were a success is because I supported her, and she supported me, and we were always in public together. We were a team."

Looking at the husband-wife dynamic through my PaPa's perspective has always helped. His kids (including my mother) were ever present at basketball, baseball, and football games. MiMi made sure his brood saw him in action as the Athletic Director. They attended all the sports games because PaPa had to be there, and MiMi believed she needed to be there, and this meant the kids were hauled to whatever event was going on any given day. It was planned togetherness based on the sports calendar. There was a sense of purpose and unity under their roof, in their station wagon, and in the stands. I think my mother's greatest blessing was to feel safe and secure, knowing that her parents were a TEAM.

PaPa believed that he and MiMi "developed a pretty good system" to keep in touch, stay emotionally bonded, and remain in each other's presence. I compare her to being a side-kick or roadie—or an ever-present angel at games and events. He once told me the following story:

"I look back and remember how Betty identified with being a coaches' wife right away. She had been a cheerleader and athlete, and that helped because right out of college I was a head basketball coach and then a head football coach. She automatically bonded with the players of all the different sports, and rode the bus with me to away games. This became important time we spent together. Or she drove to various districts in our station wagon, and put our kids in the back and followed the team.

I was gone most of the time and sometimes joked that luckily we were Catholic because it allowed me not to go to church on Wednesday night so I could spend some time at home before heading back to the office. I always talked to Betty and our family first before accepting another position and moving somewhere new. So each and every time, it became OUR plan. Wherever we went, if I hired a new coach (some right out of college), she took his wife under her wing and tutelage.

After football season we went to every school event possible. As athletic director, this meant we would be together all the time. Betty would sit at the door with me and greet people as they came in. When I first started at Waco and was head baseball coach, she told all the baseball players that she'd bake them a chocolate cake for every home run they made. We almost went broke, there were so many home runs. They did not let her off the hook, and she had chocolate cakes waiting for them at the next game. She always had a good rapport with the kids and administration.

She raised our kids by herself, and it really takes a certain type of a woman to be a good coaches' wife. She never said, 'I don't want you doing that.' She never complained about driving around in a station wagon and getting me to whatever destination I needed to be. The only complaint she ever had was that she'd occasionally overhear people saying something negative about me in the stands, and she didn't like that at all."

Teamwork in Families

My own mom, Suzanne, has a bird's eye view of what it takes to succeed as a coaching family. After all, the family is a team. By extension, moms and kids are teams, which is exemplified by the relationship she had with her mother (my MiMi).

After MiMi died, we had long conversations about the concept of growing up in the coaching lifestyle and as a family team. So much of those discussions were raw and painful simply because we were both struggling with the loss. But what came out of it were wonderful insights about what worked well. My mother was definitely raised in a loving home that involved family teamwork, and I want that for my son. What's so cool is that even though PaPa wasn't home, he really wasn't "gone" because his kids (my mother included) watched him work and knew what he did from their earliest childhoods. I plan on exposing Noah to the same philosophy.

I'm more of a "dude" kind of girl and relate well with guys, and I get this from my mom—a self-described "gym rat." Because PaPa was the head football coach and Athletic Director, he helped coach girl's basketball. My mother learned to enjoy sports from all perspectives … and became a "super athlete" in her own right. Basically, she was raised like a guy, and if there was blood or bones poking out, she shook it off. They lived on a farm when she was younger, and she had chores, like hauling hay, on top of sports. So there was no pettiness and no drama.

Her over the top competitiveness was encouraged by her parents, and her mother (MiMi) carried around her track mats and track shoes and would always try to be there for every event—again, a great example of mother-child teamwork. "Suzanne, you are so spoiled," her friends said, in awe and a bit jealous. It's no surprise that my mom did the same for me and my siblings. Writing this book has reminded me that we have always, very much, been our own family team.

Here's a funny side note. As Mom grew older, MiMi encouraged her to be feminine … but nope! She wore little hand-sewn red and velvet ruffled dresses on special occasions and looked remarkably pretty in tennis outfits. But she'd rather be in shorts. Back then they wore skirts over shorts that buttoned and unbuttoned. She wasn't supposed to remove the skirt and play in shorts, but in the back pasture, you can bet she did just that. In fact, it tickled my mom that she was taller, faster and more athletic than her brother, at least for a time. What's crazy is that my "tomboy" mom eventually designed pageant clothing and had a partnership with the pageant system! I personally think the pageant system is as competitive and ruthless as the NFL, but she was prepared for it!

Suzanne Wassermann's Story

"My mom, I think, went beyond the norm to make sure I had more time with Dad than a lot of other kids had with their fathers. And that is saying something! Our social life was a family affair tied directly to teams and games. After home games, the coaches and kids came to our house for food and desserts. Or we'd go to other coaches' homes. Sometimes there was one babysitter for all of us so the adults could mingle and we could play. We were really, truly were a family and all best friends, sitting together in the bleachers or tailgating from the backs of station wagons. We watched football practice and had picnics during practice too. I guess you could call us the 'team within the team.'

It was all interconnected, and a lot of neat lifelong friendships developed, and that segued into roles as flower girls, ring bearers and bridal attendants at weddings throughout the years. Although I was raised to be strong and capable, it wasn't always easy for me as the daughter of a coach. One thing I didn't like was the moving. I played varsity sports and did NOT want to move from Brenham to Nederland. The girls' basketball team was new (2nd year). If you played varsity and were not a senior and moved from a different school district, you had to play JV. I remember my mother tried to make everything better by letting me pick out everything I wanted for my new bedroom. My poor brother, though, was a senior— imagine how awful it must have been for him to move his senior year.

When I was a child, everyone talked about my daddy. He and his players won a lot of games, but still, even then, he couldn't make everyone happy. I occasionally overheard fans, parents, and critics saying unkind things after we lost a game. At times these things were said directly in my presence! I think the natural impulse is to defend your dad, and by extension, your family, and I had to learn to how to rein in my emotions, sort of like a politician's kid. I mastered the art of smiling and walking away. I'm just glad there wasn't social media back then because the behavior today is so bad online.

Being raised in a coaching family had its perks and drawbacks. Dad was a strong disciplinarian. I'm surprised I ever got a date because everyone at my high school held him in awe and respect. We followed the rules, period, and my mother raised us to give 110%. I remember her saying: 'If something is worth doing, we should give it our all ' I raised my kids with the same mindset. This is probably a generational 'positive' passed down through coaches' families. I've noticed that it's a different world today—kids are so privileged, and their parents fight all their battles. That didn't happen in earlier years, and I wonder why it's happening now.

It did not occur to us that we were growing up in a modest household because our friends lived similarly modest lives. Our mothers sewed, baked, gardened, canned, served homemade meals and made good use of leftovers. I know my mother did her best and always wanted better for us than what she had as a child. But most of all, she wanted us to view our family as a team, and was diligent in teaching us teamwork on the home front. "

Extended Family Dynamics

The Akins family—another branch on my family tree—honored the life of Coach Robert "Ray" Akins on January 2, 2018, and his service as a Marine and World War II veteran. I attended his funeral, remembering him as a wonderful man and famed Athletic Director and Football Coach of Gregory-Portland ISD. He was known as one of the winningest coaches in Texas for good reason, namely his 293-102-15 record. His players loved him, as did his family (and in my case, extended family). Most importantly, from 1949 onward Dorothy "Virginia" Akin was at his side, supporting him and his players and raising their three children. She is a wonderful mother and grandmother, and the best wife Coach Ray Akin could have ever asked for.

Family ties can be complicated, but as a kid it was simple. I had a notion of "family" as "all of us," not understanding how people become related through marriage or how the branches on family trees intertwined. All I knew was that somewhere, somehow, we shared roots and often celebrated togetherness at family reunions. Many of us had football as a common denominator, so as a girl growing up under the influence of sports, I thought of my great big family as a great big team, considering our Texas heritage and success on the field.

I heard legendary stories predating my birth, such as when Marty Akins, Ray's son, starred as his father's quarterback and later played for the Texas Longhorns. Both father and son are included in the Texas Sports Hall. Ray was also inducted into the Texas Coaches Hall of Fame, the Hall of Honor at Southwest Texas State University, and the Texas Coastal Bend Coaches Association Hall of Honor. He received the President Gerald R. Ford All-American High School Coach Award, and I am so proud that he accumulated 16 district titles and 17 state playoffs.

And, of course, I looked up to Ray's grandson, Drew Brees, as a 7th generation Texan and an amazing athlete, with a long career as a quarterback. You can bet I watch him play for the Saints, and already have my infant Noah doing the same. Yes, Noah is already watching football with Jeffrey and me, so I suppose he'll have the same sense of "We're a team!" and revel in our unique family dynamic.

As I wrote this book and connected with so many admirable coaches' wives, I became aware that many have their own extended family trees filled with their own lineage of athletes, coaches, and wives. Sometimes I have to wonder if it just "runs in families," and suspect that it does. But a lot of women marry into the profession without having this valuable sports background. It takes me full circle to the important concept of sisterhood and mentoring new coaches' wives as they acclimate to our culture.

Husbands, Wives and a New Program

Lisa Gotte has a great perspective on what kind of husband-wife teamwork it takes to open a new program. Her husband BJ was the former offensive coordinator at Katy High School and had played under Coach Gary Joseph in high school, so he had that long-standing tradition as well as the Katy High morals and values as inspiration. He got the job in January, and started as Paetow High's first football coach and campus athletic coordinator in February.

"It's been a really neat and unique experience to be a part of a newly built school," says Lisa. "Everything had to be established, from track, basketball, wrestling, volleyball, and the swim team. BJ had to hire every single coach, pick turf, pick every uniform, and I remember when we had football helmets stacked in the living room. He asked, 'What do you think of this one,' and 'What do you think of that one." I also helped him decide which Nike shoes and which Under Armour shoes to choose. That was certainly an example of teamwork in a coach's home."

Chapter 6: Parenting

"I believe this with all my heart: The greatest coach of all time in my eyes is my mom. She's instilled in me a toughness and a perseverance and just a never-quit mentality, and I thank her every day for providing me what she sacrificed her life for."
~ Coach Scott Brooks

*She raised our kids by herself...*these words, spoken by PaPa in the preceding chapter, got me thinking about the parenting dynamic within coaches' families. Maybe we can start with an in-depth look at pregnant-while-married-to-a-coach. Once while pregnant, I was inspired to emotionally tweet: "I am thankful for where my life is taking me, my experiences, and my relationships with others. I am thankful to be a wife, a 'mom-to-be,' and a 'mom-to-be-preneur.' But most of all, I am thankful to be able to share my faith openly and honestly."

Carrying Noah to term seemed miraculous after three miscarriages, and I was aware, more than ever, that much of the 24/7/365 parenting role would fall on me. Looking back at my pregnancy with Noah, this became crystal clear, for indeed, being a pregnant coach's wife is tough, yet beautiful. You are your own cheerleader, advocate and best friend for nine months. I have come to learn to love myself more because I HAVE TOO.

As I was sitting in my office on my yoga ball conducting a podcast, someone asked me a question that I had not thought about or put much thought into: "How are you able to do this pregnancy basically by yourself, while being in a committed marriage? Isn't that like a paradox in itself?"

Now, at that time I was a stay-at-home-while-working-mother-in-training unless traveling (which I do more than my husband). Most answers come fairly simply to me. I have always had the "you do what you have to do, no matter the situation" attitude when it comes to handling every scenario that life throws at me—including being pregnant and married to a very busy, absent, yet selfless husband due to his chosen profession (one that we BOTH LOVE deeply).

So, here is my list of "The Pregnant Coach's Wife Essentials" of the things that made my pregnancy fun and less stressful, and made my coach-husband feel less guilty for not being able to be around as much, as well!

- Find your husband's extra coaching gear that he has stowed away in his closet for years, and that you have wanted to get rid of or downsize. Then use it, yourself, while pregnant. The oversized shirts, pullovers, sweatshirts, etc., are pretty comfy pregnancy attire, and it might even make your hubby feel more "useful" and "connected" to see you in his clothes as your belly swells to massive proportions!

- Make sure your family and friends are all on the same page with the simple fact that you are basically doing this pregnancy by yourself, from moving things, to the nursery décor, to doctor's appointments, etc. (thank goodness for my mom)!

- Make time to communicate with your husband about his "to do list," which might include car seat installation, crib assembly, and toy box set up. Over the course of your second and third trimesters, he should be able to squeeze in time to do these tasks, even if he partially tackles them in sections.

- Make sure your husband has read all the books YOU wanted him to read. Make him feel a part of it as much as you can, without the guilt. Perhaps put sticky notes in the chapters that are especially vital, and highlight sections that are must-read material.

- Most of all, you have to have a great can-do mindset!

Perhaps we are given nine months of pregnancy to accomplish all the little things necessary before our children are born ... and this means that slow and steady wins the race. Don't stress—everything will get done and fall into place.

What NOT To Do

There are so many mothers of athletes out there in every conceivable type of sport, and I'm sure they use as many resources as possible to parent appropriately. Gathering insights and advice was super important to me during my pregnancy. After all, Noah was being born into a family of athletes, not to mention a coach's household. Researching how best to raise him and balance this reality consumed all of my free time. Well ... there wasn't actually a lot of free time, so I made time. I felt I owed it to my little boy and wanted to be the best mom possible.

I can thank cable programming for showing me what NOT to do. One intense reality TV show involves raising your kids to play football: The Little Tykes Series on Netflix. My blood pressure raised through the roof—it just seemed so exploitive and awful.

What To Do

But I did I strike gold on the Internet and found some GREAT advice for what I should be doing as a parent. I found a Facebook post by hockey coach Jim Traynor. He had stumbled across a sign at an ice rink in Canada that said:

"Your child's success or lack of success in sports does not indicate what kind of parent you are. But having an athlete that is coachable, respectful, a great teammate, mentally tough, resilient and tries their best IS a direct reflection of your parenting."

Wow. Just wow. I'm raising a person first and an athlete second. Noah may not play sports his whole life, but the lessons he learns while in sports will make him a better man, a better worker, and eventually a better father. And this starts with me. I promised my kiddo that I would not ever be one of the angry, obnoxious, brawling parents who disrupt games and traumatize teams by setting a horrible example. I also promised the following:

- I WILL show my son the same support my family gave me.

- I'll show up to his games, volunteer, and be his biggest cheerleader

- I'll help him process victory and defeat.

- I'll remember to teach him sportsmanship, fair play, and a work ethic.

- And I'll try not to be a clingy helicopter parent, although I totally understand the temptation to be one.

Coach's Moms

I absolutely love hearing about parenting adventure and am privileged to know coaches' wives who raised their sons into coaches. I think Susan Rodgers, Lois Faigle, and Ellie Mallory have fascinating outlooks on this topic. Coincidentally, each is the mother of three sons. Notably, Susan Rodgers and I share a connection through Drew Brees, and her son Jonny, as detailed below.

Susan Rodgers is the wife of Randy Rodgers and the mother of three remarkable sons. Moving from high school to college came suddenly, she explains. "Randy was first a head coach at a junior college in Minnesota, and I was able to stay home when the boys were little. When it was time for my middle baby to be born, I looked like I was ready to pop. Randy really wanted me to attend a convention in Atlanta, and doctor OK'd it since I had another week to go. But I went into labor and gave birth at home on the couch. Those second babies can come quickly! Thankfully, my mother was with me and called the ambulance. I'll never forget that very snowy night in Minnesota.

I'd take our boys to practices in the high school stadium. They'd do long jump hits with their sandbox, and I knew at least one or two would be coaches from the very beginning, especially when they started preparing shoe strings on cleats, organizing lockers, polishing helmets, etc. My oldest son is married, and I have one grandson who is six years old. But the NFL is far different than high school football—my son can't really take my grandson to practices. And the NFL as a whole is newer to me, coming from the collegiate level."

Susan knows a thing or two about sports injuries and adversity, and recalls that her youngest son Jonny was the star quarterback at Westlake High in Austin when her husband was recruiting for John Mackovic at the University of Texas. Drew Brees was the backup quarterback and was thinking about baseball instead of football because he didn't play much due to Jonny's presence on the field. Then an injury struck.

"Jonny tore his knee ligaments in a scrimmage, and that's when Drew became the starting quarterback," she says. The two boys remained dear friends throughout the years, and Drew became a prolific author in addition to being a notable football player. He wrote about his Westlake days and friendship with Jonny in his book Coming Back Stronger."

***

Lois Faigle, a long time friend of my grandparents, told me that life is sort of like some football seasons … lots of ups and downs. It's difficult at times, but hardships build strength. She has wonderful memories of raising her three great sons who became coaches like her husband, Jerry. She didn't know it then, but eventually they would welcome a niece who coaches basketball.

Lois gave birth to two of her sons while Jerry was on my grandfather's staff, so my grandparents got to watch her family grow. When Lois and Jerry relocated to Waller, my grandfather drove the moving truck. "My boys were all small then, but they never forgot Coach Wassermann driving that "big yellow truck."

She adds, "Each of the boys would eventually work for a short time on the Waller staff with their Dad. One of the funniest things I experienced was hearing from some high school girls that Coach Faigle was 'hot,' knowing they weren't talking about my husband! And being introduced as Coach Faigle's 'mom' felt weird the first time I heard it!"

She notes that they celebrated the victories and worked through the losses, and all the wives cherished the moments when little boys got to play with their dads when they came home

"As a coaching family, there was a difference in how we raised our children," says Lois. "Coaches we have been associated with have had high expectations of their players on and off the field, and that naturally spills over into your family expectations. I know that our boys knew they were expected to behave in such a way that their dad and their coaches would be proud."

***

Ellie Mallory is the mother of three coaches, Mike Mallory of the Jaguars, Doug Mallory of the Falcons, and Curt Mallory of Indiana State. She says her sons choose to follow in their father's footsteps because they saw what joy he had in the profession.

"I believe my sons went into coaching profession because they saw how fulfilling it was for their father to do what he loved. They saw how much good you can do working with the players."

The example of their father, Coach Bill Mallory, prepared each to coach for teams on the NFL and collegiate level. And through these experiences, they became prepared to raise their own "coaches' kids." Doug Mallory's daughters weigh in below, along with other daughters of notable coaches.

Chapter 7: Insights from Coaches' Kids

"To be around as long as I have, you have to have a good and understanding wife and a family that is totally supportive."
~ Coach Bob Hyland

Back to the incredible power of graphic t-shirts. I once saw a mother proudly wearing a shirt that said: "TRUST ME, MY SON NEVER LOSES. HE EITHER WINS OR HE LEARNS.

It got me thinking that no matter what sport Noah chooses to play (PaPa believes he should play many sports), it's his character that really matters. It also occurred to me that Jeffrey might someday coach our son in high school. That does happen in the coaching world and presents its own set of dynamics and challenges.

Watching coaches and their own children interact brings a new perspective to people who watch from the bleachers or bench. Typically, kids are there with the wives and sit together with other coach's kids. One 4th or 5th grader might become a ball boy or ball girl on the sidelines. The beautiful thing is that after the game, players get to see their coach as a father—a human being raising children. When the coach's own kiddos come out on the field after a win or loss, they are scooped into their father's arms. It's a personal moment the occurs in a very public place, but then so much of our lives are public.

***

Ellie Mallory of the AFCWA once told me that her husband coached at Bowling Green State University, Yale, Ohio State, and was the head coach at Miami University, the University of Colorado, and Northern Illinois. He finished at Indiana University, and they relocated their children throughout it all. "Our daughter Barb moved in 9th grade, and her new high school friends said, 'Boy, you make friends easily!' Barb said, 'Well, I have to!' Most kids never have to make new friends in new schools, while coaches' kids do this frequently."

Our sons have seen this through the years. It's the giving side of coaching that highlights the many worthwhile aspects that come with the job."

Ellie's son Doug, who coaches for the Falcons, married his remarkable wife, Lisa. They are parents to three daughters. Emily and Allison Mallory stare their own experiences being coaches' kids from a long line of coaches' kids:

Emily Mallory's Story

"Back in 2007, we were coaching at LSU. There were some tough fans, and sometimes even my friends would come up and say things about players and coaches that were critical. We won the national championship, which at that time was the biggest highlight of my dad's career. The win proved our team was good, and I felt vindicated.

Dad is always excited when we win and not too bummed when he comes home after a loss. This helped us keep things in perspective growing up through the highs and lows. He was fired from Indiana University when I was a sophomore at the college, and that was a rough time. Every Wednesday that season I had lunch with him at the training tables and watched the last 20 minute of practice. Him being fired after a decent season, and me still being at school, meant that I saw the negative tweets and social media posts. It was the first time we could remember him being out of a job. Two of my very best friends are coaches' kids and know exactly what that's like. Other friends may say they understand, but you really can't understand it unless you live it.

In the long run, the firing ended up being such a great thing, because Dad is now coaching with the Falcons. We went to the Super Bowl last year, and we're excited about future of the team. But whether he coached in college or now in the NFL, Dad is gone a lot. This is why coaches' wives are so strong. I saw how much Mom had to do and how she led the family. She'd pack us up and enroll us in schools. Our oldest dog, Boo, lived in six states! Our dogs, by the way, are a huge source of fun and comfort, especially after a loss. I remember that we dressed all of them up in Christmas clothes and took a million selfies with all four of them.

Our whole family managed to spend together time despite Dad's schedule. I have so many childhood memories of all five of us driving home and hanging out as a family. We'd go over the game and weigh in. That was special family time and created lots of great moments. Now that I live in Ohio, Alli lives in Louisiana, and Sarah lives in Georgia, it's a challenge to get together. It makes me appreciate those childhood experiences even more.

To some, it must seem like such a strange lifestyle because the whole world revolves around the game, but we always had fun game experiences that other kids just don't have. I feel fortunate that my dad is a coach."

Allison Mallory's Story

"Growing up, I was definitely the 'boy' of the family and knew more about football than most girls. I was the one asking why a tackle was missed, and people often told me that I should be a sideline reporter. I did start out in sports journalism but am now studying psychology as a senior at LSU. Maybe I'll go into sports psychology.

We'd always go to Dad's practices. I remember that in the 4th grade, Mom and I made cookies and I got to deliver them to Dad all by myself without my sisters. They were a huge hit, and I got to sit with Dad after practice and eat dinner with defensive coaches. And no matter where Dad was located, he had a dry erase board in his office. Every season we'd write a different note to him. He would outline it and told people not to erase it. We still do that when we visit. It's little memories like these that make me appreciate being a coach's kid. I got to do things others kids never experienced.

I remember moving to New Mexico in March because that's when the season ends. Sometimes it was fun being the 'new kid,' but the uprooting in a weird part of the year caused some problems. Classes were different and transferring credits didn't always go smoothly. In high school, we faced finals that covered material we weren't taught at our old school. The teachers didn't know what to do! I had to take a New Mexico history final and had no clue!

Moving around a lot was definitely hard, but we were excited about each new team and learning about all the new players. I moved six times before I went off to college, and it helped that I'm the middle child, because I had a younger sister and an older sister and was never alone. By the way, I met my college roommate because our dads set it up: *"You have a daughter who is about to go to LSU? ... "*

Usually, coaches' kids are friends with other coaches' kids on staff. I was glad to have that support, especially when people got upset over a game. I heard things like 'Your dad is getting fired.' I've seen upsetting tweets and the hashtag #firedougmallory. My mom would always say, 'Ignore them. They don't know what they're talking about.' I had to toughen up because I love my dad. Criticism definitely comes with the territory."

***

Another set of sisters, Gretchen and Gracie West, also come from a long lineage of football coaching talent. They are the daughters of Julie and Glenn West, and granddaughters of Shirley and Kenneth West.

Gretchen West's Story

"Since coaches are so busy, one question I'm often asked is: 'Do you miss your dad?' My answer is no because it's all I know. And plus, my dad has done a great job including me and my sister in his profession. Once he got a huge refrigerator box and put it at end of field, and let my younger sister play in it during practice. I was the ball/water girl on the sidelines for games with all the other coaches' sons. Many of the players were like brothers to me. I don't have any biological brothers, but every year I had a team of brothers.

Sports were always big for me and my sisters, and Dad enjoyed attending our games when he could. But he always said he was glad he didn't have sons because he didn't want to be our coach. He preferred cheering us on.

Dad wanted us to grow up in a small area like he did in Brownwood, and Brenham is similar. It's amazing that I spent 20 years there before going off to college and didn't have to move around like other coaches' kids. But I definitely lived in a fishbowl, which has its pros and cons. I'm thankful to have a community who knows me so well and supports me, but obviously if you mess up, everyone knows about it. In high school, I wanted to be normal like other kids. Sometimes that meant going to a party, but everyone in town was watching and the expectations for my behavior were high.

Once I went to a spring break thing, and when Dad found out I had to run a hundred miles in 20 days—five miles a day—as a consequence. Sure enough, people sat on porches and watched as Dad drove behind me, ensuring I took every step of those 20 miles. That's what we sign up for in athletics, and it shaped me for the better. I realized he's not just my dad, but also a coach to the community, a supervisor, and someone with so many roles. Dad enforced the rules for a reason.

I've been dating a guy for five years who is going to be a football coach, so I'm gearing myself up with the thought that I might have to move around a lot. He goes to UT and is interning for Westlake, and I go to TCU. His mom was my volleyball coach, and my dad was his football coach, which is neat because we got to share same emotions and feelings. It helped us battle the fishbowl aspects of it. He knows exactly what it feels like to be a coaches' kid, and he's a constant for me.

I guess through it all I really learned to tap into my family and rely on them because we are each other's support system. We know exactly what's going on in each other's lives, whereas people from the outside don't. There might be gossip from parents in town and unhappy fans since you can never please everyone all the time. So it's important to be a support system for your dad, too."

Gracie West's Story

"Dad is the AD and head football coach in Brenham It was fun growing up in a small town. I completely loved being a part of it my whole entire life. It was cool being a coach's kid and always being a part of his job. If he was a doctor or lawyer, I couldn't have been a water girl and seen him in action. We got to hang around coaches offices, and I guess that made me a super fan.

During middle school, I walked to field house and helped during practice. There were some teachable moments, like when I ordered pizza without any money and had to go to the practice field. "Dad, I need your credit card," I announced as he was right in the heat of the moment with a player. Whoops—I was sent back with no money to pay the pizza delivery man, who wasn't very happy.

I went to TCU and got my master's degree at Texas State, and am now a first grade teacher at Westlake in Austin. So I guess I've sort of followed in my mom's footprints. She used to be an art director and went back to school to become a teacher. I have to say that TCU is expensive and I was there on scholarship. People might say that teaching and coaching are not money professions, and that may be true. But there are so many other benefits to teaching and coaching. It's a calling. There's no putting on airs. Normal, average people devote their lives to these extraordinary careers. I can add that we were never spoiled, but we were never deprived, either.

A year ago I started dating a coach who coaches for my dad and used to be his quarterback. A cool story is that Michael didn't get to play much (he was really good, but the junior quarterback was better). But when the quarterback got hurt, he got to go in and throw a touchdown at the state game.

The funny thing is, I didn't date at all in high school. Guys just didn't ask me out, although I was good friends with the players. I asked Michael why that was, and he said, "Because you were off limits." I guess that went with being the coach's daughter. My grandmother, Shirley West, was like the superwoman of coaches' wives. She knew Michael, but not as my boyfriend. I know she would love that we are dating. One thing that really impressed me was that she never wanted credit and put everyone else in the spotlight. She was the glue kept us together for every holiday, every trip, and we had to re-learn how to do life after she passed.

It was such a blessing to stay in Brenham my whole life, although I never realized it until I left. The norm is to move around a lot in a coaching family, but Dad is doing well with the program, and thankfully has stayed in one place.

To other coach's kids, I say embrace it, enjoy it, and be all in there. It's really fun and the best thing in world. I was so happy that I was, and am, a coach's kid. I believe it's the best profession in the world, and if you are a coach's kid, you are pretty lucky."

***

I really enjoy talking with Paige Thurmond, who is another ultimate definition of a coach's kid. Her father, Chris Thurmond, was coaching high school football when she was an infant, and then joined the college ranks during the first fall of her life. She's able to articulate the experience so well. By the way, Chris Thurmond is a fine coach, a great person, and one of Jeffrey's mentors. Following are her insights.

Paige Thurmond's Story

"As an only child, I'm super close to my parents, who recently moved to Little Rock, Arkansas to live near me. That's a cool 'full circle' event, because I had always followed them, and now they followed me. I'm an only child, and they've been the one constant in my life.

When my father coached at University of Tulsa, I was lucky because I was able to spend the majority of my childhood around lots of family. I was a cheerleader for Salvation Army flag football in 5th grade, and my cheer friends said, 'We should go bowling after the game.' I was really surprised and asked my mom, 'People do other things on Saturday night than watch football?'

Dad took positions at Texas Christian University, Oklahoma, TCU again, Alabama, Texas A&M, University of Houston, Kentucky, and Rice. We moved during the hard ages—before 8th grade, before 10th grade, and with my parents while in college. That's the unusual takeaway from my story—I followed my parents from university to university, literally college-hopping to TCU, Alabama, and Texas A&M where I graduated with a degree in speech communication. Then it was back to Tuscaloosa for my master's degree in communication studies.

I can't speak for all coaches' kids because every situation is different. Being the kid of a head coach is different than being the kid of an assistant coach. Basketball coaches' kids have different experiences than baseball coaches' kids. But my dad and I truly bonded through football. I started grading films with Dad at age six. That way, he could share time with me and still do his job. We did this all the way through college on Sundays.

As the catering manager for Clinton Foundation, I manage 400 events a year including logistics and menu planning for weddings, corporate holidays and other happy occasions. The skills I learned from being a coach's kid enhanced my future and saved me socially in different schools because I had no choice but to be someone who attracted friends. It prepared me to work with the public.

I think it all circles back to the notion of resiliency. One universal word in a coach's kid's world is resilience. If you're not born with it, you learn it very quickly. Most kids will have some adapting to do, and there's really not a manual. I will say, however, that I developed a savant skill: knowing all the college mascots.

I'm glad there were no online message boards when I was in middle school. Armchair quarterbacks and angry fans can be so cruel with their opinions, and many have no idea what they're even talking about. Some people hide behind keyboards, and it's painful to see the depth of the negativity, especially when it's directed at someone you love or friends who are coaches.

Today when coaches lose jobs, it makes big online splashes. This doesn't happen to fathers who are architects or plumbers. The kids of architects and plumbers don't have to deal with the social media shaming and wild gossip. Coaches' kids have to be even tougher now and know how to handle the hurtful comments.

Still, with all the highs and lows, I am proud to be a coach's kid and grateful for an extraordinary childhood."

Chapter 8: The Players

"One coach will impact more young people in a year than most people do in a lifetime."
~ **Reverend Billy Graham**

One wife posted on my Facebook group, "Nothing is more heartbreaking as seeing a senior crying after a close game that we didn't win. The loss knocked us out of any hope of making the playoffs. I had one cry on my shoulder for almost 5 minutes, sweaty pads and all. I love these boys like my own."

I replied, "I understand where you are coming from. These boys are like our sons, and we love them like we would our own, and so do our husbands! All we can do is support them, be there for them, and push them to continue to grow towards the next chapter in their lives whether that be playing college football, or just continuing their education!"

This is just one among many examples of coaches' wives comforting and caring for the players. I have to remind myself that kids in golf and tennis can graduate from high school and play for leisure and enjoyment their whole lives. But most high school football players have, at most, four years on the field. Most people don't know what it means when a player's senior season ends. More than 90% will never, ever put on a helmet again. Seniors exit on a high note, or a low note, with tons of memories—and perhaps that's all. Only some go on to play college football, and even fewer make it to the professional ranks.

So coaches have a small window in which to reach their players, teach them sportsmanship and teamwork, and build them into decent human beings. As Reverend Billy Graham says, *"One coach will impact more young people in a year than most people do in a lifetime."* Some players from single-parent households might desperately need male role models. Some from privileged households might desperately need the discipline and accountability that comes with a football program. In fact, all young men need this accountability, especially if they struggle socially, academically or even athletically. The coach stands ready as an encourager and mentor.

***

I have to include insights from Dusty Vandenberg in this chapter. He is a well-known former Katy High School football lineman. I met him through my sister when they both attended the University of Houston. He works in communications for Houston icon Jim "Mattress Mac" McIngvale.

There isn't one thing about football that Dusty doesn't know—he's an encyclopedia. But what I love most about him is his gratitude toward the coaches' wives who helped and impacted him during his high school football career—and today. It demonstrates that our behind-the-scenes role means the world to some student athletes.

Dusty's Backstory

"I'm a coach's kid not because my dad coached, but because I played under Coach Gary Joseph. His wife, Sheila, raised their three kids while Coach Joseph raised hundreds and hundreds. I was one of them. When he calls you son, you become part of the Katy High football family.

I've been going to Katy High football games since I was a toddler. Coach Gary Joseph was inspirational even from the bleachers, and I wanted to play for him someday as a Katy Tiger—and be an astronaut. Fortunately for me, one of those dreams came true.

I was a true football fan—the kid who asked every football team from every high school in Katy ISD to autograph a football. I couldn't wait to play at Katy High School, which is a legendary place. My mom actually moved the family so that we were zoned there—it was that important to me academically and athletically. It's a place of dreams for aspiring players, and I knew that putting on a KATY uniform was like wearing a Superman cape. There was nothing better than wearing red and playing for the people in the stands.

Sheila Joseph, Gary Joseph's wife, is the MVP of the program. Her sons, Jon and Jeff, were coached through two State Championship ('97, '01) by their dad. Her daughter Julie is a former coach and married to Eman Naghavi, who is now the offensive line coach at the University of Louisiana Monroe. And yes, her son-in-law also played for Coach Joseph, so they are true examples of the Katy High School football program. Even today, years after graduating, I can spot Sheila Joseph's strawberry blonde hair and go over to say hello. She gives the biggest hugs and genuinely cares about the players. I always felt her support, and even though I'm long gone from the program, she still treats me like family. Once a Katy Tiger, always a Katy Tiger.

Sheila coordinated the relief effort during the Hurricane Harvey flood. Many homes in and around Old Town Katy were under water, and Coach Joseph sent players out to help the flood victims. Sheila organized it all, asking "How high was the flood in your house?" The startling fact was that her own house was flooded, but her priority was the players and the families in the community.

There are so many bittersweet memories associated with playing football. My senior year I loved country music and Carrie Underwood. We lost the State Championship game in December 2009 and Carrie Underwood got married, so I lost both dreams in two days. The Houston Chronicle covered the game and captured a picture of my reaction to the loss: 'Katy linebacker Dusty Brandenburg, center, tries to hold back tears after the Tigers' 28-17 loss to Abilene in the Class 5A Division II state high school football championship.'

When my senior season ended, I didn't know who I was. It was disorienting until I realized I was still part of the brotherhood and still part of that tradition. I had two state championship rings as well, and enrolled at University of Houston. I once mentioned to head coach Tom Herman that I played for Katy, and he said, 'Okay, you've already played college football.' There's that instant level of respect for the Katy football program."

***

Players Staying in Touch

Ellie Mallory believes that coaching is a great profession because coaches work with and are role models for young people. "We've been out of business quite a few years, and our former players are all grown men, but there's a bond between coaches and players who fought battles together, a very strong bond. They still look at Bill and I as the coach and the coach's wife. We are still in touch with some of them from decades ago," she says.

"Some of the players have had to deal with life issues, such as marital problems and illnesses. I remember when one lost a child," she recalls. "You just step in and try to help—and that's not in the contract. The wives are fondly remembered as kind and supportive encouragers."

***

Susan Rodgers told me she couldn't afford babysitters, so some of the football players became babysitters. "We've been out of coaching business for quite a few years, and some of our former players are grown men in their 50s. But they still look at us as 'coach and coach's wife,' and they still talk about those babysitting stints at reunions. Time certainly flies, but these memories are forever."

***

Rhonda Clayton notes how remarkable it is to experience the dynamic between coaches and players, and witness how these special relationships grow into decades-long bonds. She taught many of the future football players in elementary school, saw them coached in high school by her husband Don, and also watched many perform in college games. Due to this unique bond, she and Don have been invited to many weddings of former players.

***

The coaching community was shaken when Shirley West passed away. Shirley had married Kenneth West when he coached at Brownwood under Gordon Wood, the "winningest high school football coach in the nation." According to her daughter-in-law Julie West, they won many state championships and were feverish for sports. "With only three coaches on staff, this meant three wives organized the moms' clubs and fan clubs, and brought everyone together to create a family atmosphere," she says.

Shirley was a founding member of the Texas High School Coaches Wives Association. She and Kenneth opened their homes to new coaches who transferred in. Not only the coaches' wives, but the players themselves, remember Shirley's kindness and graciousness. Anyone who had played under Coach Kenneth West was touched by her helpfulness and inclusiveness, and many posted on her online obituary with comments like, "Such a nice lady! Our youngest son was treated like a special person by Mrs. West. We will have wonderful memories of her. We send our sincere sympathy to your family," and "My heart just breaks at the loss of Shirley. I am so glad that I got to visit with her when I was in Texas last month. Growing up the way I did, I was raised by more than just my own parents. Those Brownwood coaches and their wives were the village that raised a lot of us, and for that I thank God every day. Shirley always looked out for me and took such great care of me, and I loved her very much. Know that you all are in my prayers."

Julie told me that Shirley was more than a mother-in-law. "She was truly like my own mother, and I adore and miss her so badly, I can't even tell you. I was able to stand at her funeral among many, many coaches' wives and honor her. Everyone misses Shirley—all the wives she mentored, all the players she encouraged, and of course my daughters Gretchen and Gracie."

***

Likewise, many kind comments, some from former students and athletes, were included on MiMi's obituary page and on social media. One said, "I played high school baseball for Coach Wassermann, and his wife would always bake a cake for the player who hit a home run. I remember Coach and Mrs. Wassermann very fondly. Super people." Another said, "Dear Coach, our heartfelt sympathies go out to you. Many, many thanks to you & Mrs. W. for all you've done over the years … not just building young athletes but young adults. May God's grace comfort in coming days. You will be in our prayers."

Teresa Combe said," She LIVED to give and encourage and support others! I was incredibly blessed to be on the receiving end of all of her love and nurturing. She (and Lloyd) made all the difference in the world in my life." Laurie Corbelli, former Texas A&M volleyball Coach, said, "Lots of prayers for the Wassermanns. We are so grateful that MiMi came into our lives, and for what she (and Lloyd) did to shape the lives of our children. She will be greatly missed by all of us." PaPa's player from the 1970s, Gordon Ray LeBlanc, reached out to say, "We were welcome at the Wassermann house 24/7. Mrs. W. definitely gave up a lot of her time with Coach so that he could be studying film and preparing our team for the games each week."

Chapter 9: Texas High School Football is Epic

"Football is to Texas what religion is to a priest."
~ Coach Tom Landry

First off, football is a Texas way of life. I will try to explain this phenomenon to people who may not live in Texas, because, as Coach Tom Landry says, "Football is to Texas what religion is to a priest."

Texans certainly enjoy collegiate and pro football, but it's the high school football games that pull moms, dads, siblings and entire towns onto the bleachers. Yes, high school football is epic around here. If you are a transplant from another state, you might question this football fanaticism. Over time it seeps into your pores and enters the bloodstream. Any Texas high school graduate has been exposed to this virus via pep rallies, spirit wear, and mascots. Many spend Friday nights in the stands or on the field cheering a team on. I don't care if you are in FFA, Student Council or the French Club … chances are, you showed up at least once or twice for the home team.

Our state shines a light on this great, big production known as Texas high school football. We all know high school football exists in other states, but in Texas it is glamorized, and I once wrote an article to that effect, noting that "Friday Night Lights" is a culture that has been celebrated for 90 years. Books have been written, sports journalists have weighed in, magazines have covered the phenomenon, movies have been made, and television shows have been produced showcasing its commodity.

I should know … my talented cousin Michael Waxman directed episodes of NBC's Friday Night Lights television series, which is truly spot on. My husband won't watch it because he says it's like reliving his day from our sofa (he needs his downtime, as rare as it is). But the series is one of my absolute favorites and has millions of fans. Cousin Michael undertook an interesting journey from his native Brooklyn, New York to Bastrop, Texas where he lives today. Some of the Friday Night Lights filming occurred at the Del Valle High School football stadium in Travis County, Texas.

Okay, I have to brag a bit about Michael, who is one huge inspiration in the entertainment business. He studied television and film production, worked with Fred Rogers (from Mr. Rogers' Neighborhood) on a series called Old Friends, New Friends, became a production assistant, and worked on commercials, documentaries, TV shows, and major motion pictures. He's known for When Harry Met Sally, Parenthood, Prime Suspect, Grimm, Once Upon a Time, 12 Monkeys, and more projects than I can rattle off. He met his wife Linda as they both worked on the movie Manhunter. She's an Austin native, and they decided to raise a family in Bastrop (right outside of Austin) rather than in Los Angeles. So he commutes to California for work. I think this is why he can definitely empathize with coach-husbands who aren't on the home front a lot.

So what can coaches' wives learn from watching Friday Night Lights? If you are familiar with Brett and Kate McKay's "Art of Manliness" blog like I do, you're probably familiar with the concepts from the show that they so accurately and eloquently lay out regarding the iconic television series:

- The underdog role is relished

- Manliness is nurtured

- Redemption is sought

- Texas is forever

- A man's closest ally is his wife (I love this!)

- A man needs a team

- Clear eyes and full hearts can't lose

Football as Glue

As for coach's wives who are new to this culture, I believe football really *is* the glue that oversteps differences and unites people to become one. Here are some quick facts. There are a guaranteed 10 games. Six rounds of playoffs determine the right to become 1 of the 10 state champions in the five 11-man classifications. December means it could quite possibly be the last time some student athletes ever step foot on the field as a competitor. A State Championship leads to some nice bling on your finger, post season accolades, and quite possibly movement amongst the staff.

So Texas high school football is more than just an athletic period, and Friday night under the lights is a business. Jeff Fleener, head coach at Brandeis High School in San Antonio, once tweeted: "Everyone recruits Texas, so if you don't recruit them, you're playing against them." Isn't that the truth? There are more than 1 million high school football players who will accumulate statistics that help determine their chances of competing at the college level, and ultimately the professional level, but only if the shoe fits.

In Texas there are more 5A and 6A schools comprised in the shortest of distances than any other highly recruited surrounding state. In these last four years, the Lone Star State has had more than 35 players consecutively in the "Top 300" 247Sports' composite rankings. Texas ranks #1, averaging over 340 Football Bowl Subdivision (FBS) contenders each year, which means annually they produce enough players to fill about 18 recruiting classes.

Small Talk

If you're ever at an event, social function, or conference and need some additional fast facts or conversation starters, the following trivia might help.

- Girls—I call them the "Gridiron Girls"—do play on some Texas high school football squads. Oh yes, they do. These are not fictional Lucy Draper-type characters played by Kathy Ireland in the movie Necessary Roughness. No, these are actual student athletes, like the amazing K-Lani Nava, who on December 20, 2017 as a Strawn High School kicker, made history as the first female to score in a Texas Class 1A Division II Six-Man state championship game—at 5'3" and weighing 140 pounds! Trevion Borders is another female football player who blazed a trail as a Klein Oak high freshman. Maya Ochoa played wide receiver and safety as a freshman at Creekview High. Sophomore Evonnie Ramos played TV as a left guard and special teams in Fort Stockton. The numbers fluctuate, but when I last checked there were more than 150 high school females playing football in Texas compared to roughly 160,000 boys.

- Some say football is a gladiator sport, complete with coliseums. I say this is accurate if you look at the structures being built to accommodate fans, equipment, and the players. 1,305 high school football stadiums exist in Texas. But don't blink—more are being built. Guess how many have been erected since 2010 … 60 and counting! Some are HUGE! Toyota Stadium in Frisco seats 20,500. Memorial Stadium in Mesquite seats 20,000. Alamo Stadium in San Antonio seats 18,500. Farrington Field in Fort Worth seats 18,500. Allen Eagle Stadium in Allen seats18,000. Buccaneer Stadium in Corpus Christi seats 18,000. Ratliff Stadium in Odessa seats 17,900. San Angelo Stadium in San Angelo seats 17,500. Stallworth Stadium in Baytown seats 16,500. Burger Stadium in Austin seats 15,000.

- The mums. Oh my Lord, the mums. It's another "Texas thing," and every year Homecoming becomes a clavicle-to-ankle pageant of pomp and floral artistry. What started as simple, fresh chrysanthemum corsages in the 1950s (MiMi's heyday) morphed into pounds of bling and ribbon (and sometimes LED lights)—a gargantuan spirit bouquet worn on the chest, and the bigger, the better. Yes, the weight of it can tear holes in clothing. Yes, they now come in necklace-halter styles. The guy gives his girl a mum made either by his mom or a professional mum designer, and the girl gives her guy a coordinating flower-laden garter to wear on his sleeve. That way, they are properly matched & mummed as befitting a Texas high school couple at a homecoming dance, and afterward, the mums end up as décor on bedroom walls. The goal for some is to eventually collect four—one for each year in high school.

- You become the mascot (sort of the opposite of personification and anthropomorphism, for all you wordsmiths out there). Your "sports identity" is tied to an animal or thing or whatever your team happens to be named for. You are a lion, tiger, bear, armadillo, skeeter, stingaree, goat, or gobbler, because your team is called the Dublin Lions or the Katy Tigers or the West Brook Bruin Bears or the San Saba Armadillos or the Mesquite Skeeters or the Texas City Stingarees or the Groesbeck Goats or the Robert E. Lee Ganders. It is what it is—an intense pride in something symbolic and unifying (that glue notion again). Logos, jackets, t-shirts, megaphones, pendants, bumper stickers, and occasionally earrings are all components of this Texas mascot magic. Of course, "Who stole the mascot" is a whole other type of game played between feuding rivals.

Coaching

Eight FBS schools in Texas have hired a former Texas high school football coach on their staff as full-time assistants. In Texas, high school football is as competitive as college football, with some schools bigger than most smaller universities. The coaches are just as, if not better than, most collegiate coaches. Their programs are highly formulated and include teaching nutrition, proper weight training techniques, and daily drills. All of this lets the athletes, parents, and administration know they are getting a very skilled coach and a very well-coached football player.

David Beaty, a Kansas football coach, says of Texas coaching talent: "They are ridiculously good coaches. You could fill a lot of college staffs with coaches in that state." Bringing former high school coaches on staff is frequent in Texas. The connections they make while attending clinics and conventions, and the unity itself for being a coach in Texas, speak volumes. There are several head coaches such as David Beaty, Art Briles, Todd Graham, Mike Jinks, Philip Montgomery and Chad Morris who have made it to the next level. In fact, Briles hired four Texas high school coaches to his staff for his first head coaching job at the University of Houston. They ended up at the Conference USA Championship.

The leadership in charge of college programs know what's going on within the high school programs in Texas. It's that important. But recruiting isn't the only factor and communication is key. The high school coaches in the state of Texas are great teachers. They understand the importance of molding the student-athlete who understand the sophistication of it all. The goal is to produce young men can compete athletically and academically. The coaches, themselves, are generally excellent communicators in the classroom, on the field, and while being looked at as a possible recruits to the college ranks, themselves.

The heady, dizzying aspects of winning can't be denied. Winning is a very public event. Winning streaks build a swell of emotion and expectations on the home front and in the stands. The man you are married to becomes a hero and everyone loves him until … there's a defeat. It's never fun when the mood in the stands becomes anguished, or even vicious. It helps when I think of MiMi, who kept her dignity even when PaPa lost a critical game and the world temporarily crashed around them.

It's a cycle of the highest highs and lowest lows. My husband Jeffrey has this to say about the never-ending saga: "Win," "No Excuses," "Play Like a Champion," and "Losing Sucks." When he watches games, he generally roots for the team behind in points and then will switch when that team takes the lead. Why? Because there is nothing worse than the feeling of losing, especially a bowl game or championship game. He lost a state championship, and it haunted him for years. It reminds me of the saying by Terry Pratchett: "Always remember that the crowd that applauds your coronation is the same crowd that will applaud your beheading." So Jeffrey really, truly feels for the players, especially during the Fox Sports presentation of the Texas high school football championship (mentioned below).

Jeffrey also says, "With every winner, there is also a loser. Half the teams in the country lose that day. It is a two-team game, and that's simple math." With defeat comes life lesson and teachable moments and character-building challenges. It's all about developing players into better versions of themselves and creating relationships. Shoot, one of his players from years ago flew in for our wedding, and others arrived by car!

Jeffrey wants to win, and defeat is heartbreaking. He mentioned once that it would be GREAT for new wives to understand how layered and complicated defeat can be.

The Media Knows the State

Last December 14–17, 2016, FOX Sports Southwest provided live webcasts of the UIL Six-Man championship games AND live Television coverage of the 2016 UIL Texas High School Football State Championships from AT&T Stadium. People love the players and want to know where they come from and where they're heading, especially the rare few who jumped straight into the NFL. It's true that collegiate football certainly provides a great pool of talent for the NFL, but high school football has also occasionally contributed to the league.

Just off the top of my head (and I'm leaving out more than 100 pros), the following Texas high school players went big:

- The Denver Bronco's Von Miller played at Desoto High.

- The San Francisco 49ers' Tony Jerrod-Eddie played at

Desoto High.

- The New Orleans Saints' Mike Murphy played at Desoto High.

- The Baltimore Ravens' Zachary Orr played at Desoto High.

- The Baltimore Ravens' Justin Tucker played at Westlake High.

- The New Orleans Saints' Drew Brees played at Westlake High.

- The Philadelphia Eagles' Nick Foles played at Westlake High

- The Baltimore Ravens' Ryan Mallett played at Texas High.

- The Oakland Raiders' Derek Carr played at Clements High.

- The Indianapolis Colts' Andrew Luck played at Stratford High.

- The Kansas City Chiefs' Derrick Johnson played at Waco High.

- The Dallas Cowboy's Dez Bryant played at Lufkin High.

- The New York Jets' Josh McCown played at Jacksonville High.

- The New York Jets' Bryce Petty played at Midlothian High.

- The Washington Redskins' Trent Williams played at Longview High.

- The Seattle Seahawks' Earl Thomas III played at West Orange-Stark High.

- The Detroit Lions' Matthew Stafford played at Highland Park High.

- The Tampa Bay Buccaneers' Mike Evans played at Ball High.

- The Cincinnati Bengals' Andy Dalton played at Katy High.

- The Miami Dolphins' Ryan Tannehill played at Big Spring High.

- The Cleveland Browns' Johnny Manziel played at Tivy High.

- The good news is that anyone lacking football knowledge can educate themselves online. So, wives, what are some of the best sources for high school football news? The following are some of my favorites:

- Dave Campbell's Texas Football (texasfootball.com/)

- Texas High School Football (texashsfootball.com/)

- Old Coach FNF magazine (fnfmagazine.com/texas/)

Television and Big Screen

I have to mention Coaches' Wives–a documentary film. This production is just fabulous and includes a variety coaches' wives in a variety of sports. Of special interest to football families, it features Carolyn Allen, wife of Coach Randy Allen of Highland Park High School; Neezer McNab, wife of Coach Joe McNab of Notre Dame High School; and Angie Wilks, wife of Coach Dean Wilks of Lincoln County High School. If you have a chance, check it out at coacheswivesdoc.com. The documentary gives such a great overview of the experiences we all share regardless of the sports teams our husbands coach.

Earlier I mentioned the Friday Night Lights TV series, and there's also a 2004 movie by the same name directed by Peter Berg and starring Billy Bob Thornton, based on a book written in 1990 by H. G. Bissinger titled: Friday Night Lights: A Town, a Team, and a Dream. So to all the coaches' wives who love book adaptations, I recommend all of the above.

In fact, you'll find quite a few family-friendly selections of football-themed movies that you can watch with your kids. But it's always a good idea to verify beforehand that the films are appropriate for younger or older children. Jeffrey says that Remember the Titans reminds him of me, because as a little kid I knew more about football than most parents did. And he calls Little Giants a cute Pop Warner movie. Other greats include the Game Plan, Gus, The Long Shots, Invincible, Radio, Rudy, Undefeated and The Blindside.

Speaking of The Blindside, although Hollywood tends to "jazz up" football, both Jeffrey and I agree that it's a cool movie on many levels. I like that it starred an offensive lineman who was born into poverty, saved by a compassionate mother, and ultimately won Super Bowl XLVII in 2013. Jeffrey likes that the main character has such a large frame—a gentle giant who became a tough and effective player. It reminds him of a famous Pro Football Hall of Fame speech in which Russ Grimm says of his coach:

> "He told me that playing offensive line, there's no greater feeling than to be able to move a man from Point A to Point B against his will. I tried it; I liked it; and I was playing offensive line [in a] real soft and quiet demeanor, [and] had to be told it's okay to be violent. So big, so young, not allowed to play with babies, don't hurt this person, that person ... [you] grow up being really soft, and then it clicks and you get to be big and strong."

All the football movies I've enjoyed are too numerous to list, but below are some that are highly "educational," or at least eye-opening. The Program starring Halle Berry and James Caan is my favorite. Jeffrey thinks that Any Given Sunday starring Cameron Diaz, Al Pacino, and Jamie Foxx is incredibly accurate. As a kid growing up, he watched Necessary Roughness and still remembers the quote from Evander Holyfield, who made a cameo appearance in the movie as the Convict Football Player: *"I don't feel so good. I think I swallowed a finger."*

Here's our list of recommendations:

- Draft Day starring Kevin Costner

- The Replacements starring Keanu Reeves and Gene Hackman

- Brian's Song starring Dick Butkus, James Caan, and Billy Dee Williams

- Everybody's All-American starring Jessica Lange, John Goodman, and Dennis Quaid

- Gridiron Gang starring Dwayne Johnson

- Semi-Tough starring Burt Reynolds, Kris Kristofferson, and Brian Dennehy

- We Are Marshall starring Matthew McConaughey

- Invincible starring Mark Wahlberg

- Paper Lion starring Alan Alda

- North Dallas Forty starring Nick Nolte, Charles Durning, and Dabney Coleman

- Varsity Blues starring Paul Walker, John Voight, and James Van Der Beek

- Leatherheads starring George Clooney, Renée Zellweger,

and John Krasinski

- Remember the Titans starring Ryan Gosling, Denzel Washington, and Hayden Panettiere

So the media, whether it be in sports journalism or the entertainment industry, broadcasts just how much people fall in love with football. It's a national pastime and certainly a Texas high school obsession, and it's never too late to learn more about the game while snacking on popcorn and watching movies from your couch (if you happen to have an hour or so of downtime to spare).

Chapter 10: I Wish You Knew

"Everyone needs a coach. It doesn't matter whether you're a basketball player, a tennis player, a gymnast or a bridge player."
~ Bill Gates

It's true that coach's wives can, and do, become friends with non-coach's wives. These friendships expose us to a strange new world, where husbands are home early every evening because they work 40-hour weeks. I can't even imagine it. So when these friends complain that their husbands work five hours of overtime, I secretly think, *Aren't you lucky! Mine works five hours of overtime every single day. Except it's not considered overtime. It's his job.*

It's not just the unpaid hours that are an issue. Unlike coaches, most corporate husbands are not in the arena facing foes and fierce crowds. I once saw a meme that said, *"Screaming at the coaches and players won't make them perform any better. Shut up and go get some nachos. You'll feel better soon."* Hasn't every coach's wife wanted to say that at one time or another?

Seriously, verbal abuse and public scrutiny are just one part of the challenges our coach-husbands deal with. I called this chapter the "I Wish You Knew" chapter because it describes exactly what our husbands go through to earn a paycheck. They aren't doing this for the money. They are doing this for the kids. They are not paid for all the hours they put in (not even remotely close). I think if you numerically explored a coach's salary, you would discover that they actually make cents on the dollar based on all the time they devote to the classroom, the field, the profession, and the players.

Sure, coaches say things like, "Practice like you've never won. Perform like you've never lost," and "First downs to touchdowns, that's how we roll," and other motivational quips. But the bottom line is that many coaches do so much more than motivate. They willingly step in to fill whatever void a player faces, and this nurturing is done out of the goodness of their hearts. They care, and it's a calling—a ministry to some. It's one of the many unpaid things they do to make our communities (and our world) a better place.

Capturing the Sentiment

Oh, how I wish everyone knew just what it takes to be a coach and why they give so much to their players and programs. Kristin Antill Bourgeois, wife of Coach Jason Bourgeois, so eloquently captured this sentiment and shared it on Facebook a few years back. With her permission and through her inspiration, I wrote my own version for my blog, as shown below:

- I wish you knew the hours upon hours of prep that goes on before your kid ever steps foot on campus, because you'd have a whole new appreciation for coaches at the beginning of the school year.

- I wish you knew that the focus on next season starts literally the day after the current one ends.

- I wish you knew that while he may be the head coach of a certain sport, in most cases, he is required to coach a second one. This means that for our family, in the span of one year, there are on average 14 weeks out of the year where he's not working 60-80 hours per week. In other words, when we can be a "normal" family. That number decreases by one the further we make it into football playoffs each year. So while we are faithfully cheering on our football team week after week, know that we are sacrificing precious family time with every win. We cheer anyway because we love these kids and believe in them. We believe in the program.

- If only you understood that we, his family, are waiting for sometimes our first hug of the day while you discuss what type of t-shirts you want the program to order this season.

- There are many mornings my husband wakes up before 5 am to go pick up an athlete who would not make it to morning lift without a ride, and on the other week days still manages to leave before any of us are up for the day. Those are the same days he may come home after we are in bed for the night.

- I wish you knew that even during those 80 hour weeks, there are other responsibilities such as booster clubs, fundraisers, budgets, equipment orders, and other things to manage. Phone calls are never ending. He takes the time to answer them and listen because it's his job to do so.

- Did you know that most likely your coach is also a teacher? There are lesson plans to be prepped, papers to grade, classes to teach, and students to manage. I wish you knew how many times he's voluntarily given up conference periods for athletes.

- I wish you knew that if he's hard on your kid, pushes them, expects more, it's because he knows they are holding back. THEY WILL thank him for this one day.

- I wish you knew that as hard as he may appear, I've seen him help kids out who are in trouble in the middle of the night, counsel kids at parents' requests who just wouldn't listen, and be a trusted ear when they need someone to talk to. I've seen him coach kids who were drafted, kids who would never touch a football again after high school, lose kids in accidents, and everyone in between. He would drop everything in a heartbeat if your son really needed him. He LOVES them all.

- I wish you knew the sacrifices his own children make so that he can work with your sons. I wish you knew that when our girls were younger, I worried a lot about them resenting him for this. I've learned, however, that they are so proud of their dad and they rejoice in his victories and their hearts break with his defeats.

- I wish you knew, though, that he will never get to coach his own little boy's t-ball team, soccer team, or football team most likely—not until his son in high school if he continues to play.

- I wish you knew how much that hurts him.

- I wish you knew that we, his family, hear the insults from the stands, the second-guessing because you obviously know more than he does. We read the social media jabs and hear about the aggressive emails. We smile anyway because that's what we are supposed to do. We try not to take it personally. I wish you knew how hard it is to do that. But we do it anyway. Because it's the right thing to do.

- Your coach was hired as a professional and has a proven track record of success in his career. I wish you knew that despite this he is constantly being criticized to his players by men who don't coach High School Football for a living. In fact, I wish you knew they assume he must know nothing because he coaches high school football for a living.

- I wish you would remember this man is a son, a husband, a father, a brother, an uncle, a friend, a colleague. I wish you knew he obviously doesn't do this job for the money or the recognition. He does it because he loves the game, he loves kids, and he loves what the sport teaches them about life. I wish you knew he prays for your kids, and your families. Our family does too. All of us.

- I don't have any agenda for this except to remind those outside the coaching world to stop and think about these men as what they are: Human. They aren't perfect. Are you? They make mistakes. They own up to them. They rejoice in your sons' triumphs, and they hurt when they are hurt.

- I wish you knew they are honestly doing the best that they can. And I wish you knew that just one positive affirmation for all of this can keep them going when exhaustion has left them hanging on by a thread.

- More importantly, and most of all, I hope you know how much he loves this job.

Side Jobs

You've heard of police officers who work off-duty security for events, right? Well, coaches often work side jobs as well, adding to their already overwhelming schedules. Their teaching and coaching duties might be fulfilling, but the salary doesn't always cover the bills. Perhaps they have a son starting college or a daughter getting married. Maybe they need to save extra money for retirement.

Is it any wonder that Jeffrey tutors and offers private lessons? He also followed his entrepreneurial spirit and developed a football app— the "SidelinesCoach" App—that has become quite popular simply because it's highly effective. I'm so proud of him!

Best of all, the app was finalized on December 8, 2017, the day our son Noah was born. Talk about a milestone moment both personally and professionally! Jeffrey rolled it out with a "The Most Important Document of My Coaching Career" announcement and an explanation of how the app works. I'm sharing it because I admire him so much for developing it:

Purpose of the 2 pt App:

Simple Math is not easy. At least not when you have a headset on, trying to make adjustments, talking to anywhere between five and fifteen young men, and all the while listening to three to five other coaches talking through the headset.

When your team is driving the field it is typically easy to decide what to do: kick the extra point or Go For 2. However, when you just scored and the other team is driving and you need to add zero, three, six, seven or even eight to their score, you now need to add six to yours, then go to "The Card."

This interactive scoreboard allows the fans to predict the future as well as the coach to take matters in his own hands and not worry about having three or more coaches in the box figuring out what you need to do next.

Purpose of Run/Pass by Down and Distance:

State! So much of this game is about statistics which lead to tendencies. Defensive coordinators are trying to get a beat on what teams run by down and distance, personnel and formations. At the same time, offenses are trying to stay balanced and not "show their hand."

As a fan and as a coach, the amount of times I've noticed the imbalance of throwing on 1st down or always running on 3rd and short is immeasurable and significantly valuable.

As a staff, this app allows you to track the very basic play call in football and can be comparable to "fastball vs offspeed pitch on a 3-2 count." As coaches, we chart our play calls, but we have no live stats.

As a fan, you now get to see how the offensive came is being called, predict calls, make bets with your buddies and most importantly second guess the coach. What a great way to make the game interactive.

How to Use the SidelinesCoach App:

The interactive scoreboard allows fans to see what is going to happen throughout the course of a game.

As a coach, this allows you to continue to do your job with all the math and decisions and the infamous "card" all in one place.

Keep up with the score live or throw the numbers on the scoreboard real quick, right before the head coach asks, "What are we doing? Are we going for 2?"

Your team is up 30-28. Defense is on the field. You need to know NOW what you are going to do if they score. If they kick a field goal to take a 1 point lead and you score your 6, "What do you do?" Up 5 go for 2. If they score 6 and kick the extra point, then what? So many scenarios, so little time. You don't have time to calculate all of these with so many other things to do.

Chapter 11: Once a Coach's Wife, Always a Coach's Wife

"There ought to be a special place in heaven for coaches' wives."
~ Coach Bear Bryant

I have enjoyed sharing this deep and thoughtful "behind the scenes" look an array of coaches' wives at the high school, college, and pro level. Each has her own approach to navigating the lifestyle, whether in an active coaching environment or retired. I can't help but include some additional parting reflections by veteran wives who I admire and respect as contemporaries of my MiMi. Some have husbands who segued into other professions, yet exemplify the notion that "Once a coach's wife, always a coach's wife." Robin Cook and her husband Lee did just that, and her story is fascinating.

Robin Cook

Robin is another dear friend of my Wassermann grandparents. In fact, it was PaPa who said, "You have to interview Robin Cook. She really exemplifies what it is to be a coach's wife." When PaPa hired her husband, MiMi took Robin under her wing. Robin was brand new to the coaching life, and I love her perspective as someone who left the coaching profession, but stayed connected to the culture. Robin is a retired school teacher whose husband became a banker after coaching three years.

"It was very hard leaving Lloyd and Betty Wassermann when Lee changed careers," says Robin. "Lloyd was head coach and AD when I was a cheerleader, and he and Betty became close with my parents. Lee played at TCU and earned his master's degree, and then Lloyd brought him on board. He and Betty became our support system when we were newly married and didn't know many people. Betty really stepped in when our first daughter was born. She took care of Courtney while I taught in the classroom. The team had been struggling, and Lloyd turned it around. The coaches' wives wanted to do their part by wearing matching t-shirts. I'll never forget that feeling of being part of a big family.

Lee accepted a banking position in his home town, but we always had an interest in football and football programs. So when moved back to my hometown of Brenham, Lee jumped into being involved with our coaching friends. We lived across the street from the field house. On Sundays in the neighborhood, the coaches shared meals as they reviewed films and got ready for the week. We began providing barbecue, casseroles, and other meals, which Lee took to the coaches. We did this for about fifteen years every Sunday night. It kept Lee connected to his coaching buddies and me connected to the wives. It brings to mind the saying, 'Once a coach, always a coach,' but also 'Once a coach's wife, always a coach's wife.' The same feeling of family and support existed, even though Lee wasn't coaching on the field.

Brenham brought in Glenn West as athletic director and head football coach after Lloyd Wassermann left. Glenn and Lee became best friends. I remember Glenn always saying, 'What's cooking down there?" Glenn's wife Julie and I became best friends, and our daughters are friends, as well. And just as Betty Wassermann babysat for me, I babysat for Julie's children so she could teach in school. In fact, the first time I watched Julie's children, Julie and Glenn were brand new to the program, and we didn't really even know each other. But that's what's so special about the family atmosphere. We trusted each other, depended on each other, and stepped up to help. That's what coaches' wives do.

Lee and I rarely missed a football game. Even after my girls went to college and married, Julie invited me to attend games with the coaches' wives. Once it's in the blood, it's always there—the desire to support the team at home and away games."

Julie West

Just as PaPa had urged me to interview Robin, now it was Robin's turn to say, "You have to interview Julie West. She's an amazing coach's wife." And so I reached out to Julie, who I've mentioned previously in the book. Just as Robin promised, I quickly realized that Julie is the epitome of a coach's wife and has such a funny and heartwarming story. Part of that story involves her mother-in-law Shirley West, who was another trailblazer for coaches' wives.

"My husband was named Gordon Glenn West for a reason. His father, Kenneth West, was at Brownwood with famed Coach Gordon Wood. Kenneth happened to be there with Gary Joseph's dad, Eddie Joseph. So I married into quite a football family.

I married Glenn when I was twenty-four and remember Robin saying, "Let's get started!" and showing me how to make huge pots of chili. She said, 'It's late and the guys are tired, but they are so wanting to talk about the game.' It might be 10:30 at night with little children running around, but we all enjoyed that late night chili. Those were glorious years, and during my twenty-seven years of marriage I attended every home game.

I was just swept off my feet by Glenn. I recall thinking, 'Yay! I'm in love with a guy who wears stretchy pants— burnt orange stretchy bell bottom coaching pants!' I knew nothing about the coaching life, but was crazy about him. I knew he had a vision. Twenty-seven years later, I have to say this has been more fun than I could have ever imagined. I wouldn't trade the heartaches and joys, the kids and families, for anything in the world.

Glenn is the past president Texas High School Coaches Association (THSCA), a governing body that shares the love of coaching. If you say yes to the association, you buy into the profession legislatively and the importance of coaching children. But the organization and membership also care about the individual coach, his family, and how he conducts his life. These are men and women of character. So through the THSCA, Glenn and I got to be a part of coaching all over Texas."

Susan Rodgers

Susan is an extraordinary coach's wife and coach's mother. She met Randy Rodgers 45 years ago when she was a teacher, and he was a junior high coach. Her three sons all played football. Below is her unique perspective on what the role of a coach's wife (and a coach's mother) entails.

"I've been married 45 years and initially thought my husband, Randy, would always be a junior high head football coach at a small school. I recall volunteering at those early games. I sold tickets, popped popcorn, and helped with concessions. We drove used cars and bought used furniture, and didn't notice the difference. With three boys, there was no sense buying anything new anyway. When the boys entered school, I was a teacher and had their same schedule. Still, it was a challenge to meet everyone's needs. I depended on other coaching families and staff, and vice versa. They became our best friends and a surrogate family, always pitching in.

My advice to younger coaches' wives is to accept that your marriage is not a 50/50 deal. In our world, it's closer to 95/5, and you are in charge of everything. If you can do anything to make your husband's life easier, that's part of your role. Once I heard a younger wife say, 'I unpacked my clothes and he can unpack his…' and I thought, 'Uh oh. There might be some problems with that philosophy.' Just remember that your husband is coaching for you too, and that's how he financially supports you and the family.

Also, always believe in your husband. Don't doubt him. Be supportive. It's a family profession. And it's a profession that deeply impacts young men who grow into older men. One of my husband's old players went through open heart surgery and was afraid he wouldn't pull through. He told my husband that he loved him and thanked him for being his coach. Our husbands really do affect young men and build their character.

I think it's great that Erica has written this book. It's important to look at our roles through the eyes of many coaches' wives. Last year when my son Jeff happened to walk past Erica at a Chicago Bears' game, her husband said, "Hi." Erica said, "Do you know who that is?" Her husband wasn't sure, and she said, "That's Jeff Rodgers." I got such a kick out of that story and admire Erica's grasp of the teams, the coaches, and the players from high school to the NFL."

Lois Faigle

I previously mentioned Lois Faigle, a friend of the family with ties to my Wassermann grandparents for decades. I asked her to contribute some insights for this book, and what she shares is familiar, nostalgic, comforting, and validating:

"My family lived in the Brenham area. Dad ran a barbershop for over 50 years and Mom was a school nurse. We had a large family and lots of chores to do. I aspired to be a teacher which I eventually accomplished. I later got my masters in counseling and an elementary position from which I retired in 2014.

I had no idea what to expect when I married a coach. I was alone a lot at first. Jerry and I were still newlyweds when we moved to Brenham, where we met the Wassermann family. As the "rookie" of the Brenham wives, I learned a lot from watching Betty. I was impressed that she took the time to go to football practices, got to know the players personally, knew all the coaches and their wives (of course), and managed her home and family—all with a smile on her face!

Football games became my "social life," and I rode Betty her to some of the out of town games. We didn't always get there on time. We got lost sometimes, even with her having gotten directions from her husband beforehand. But she laughed her way through it, telling us he'd be looking for us in the stands during the national anthem!

Betty was a unique head coach's wife, compared to what I've experienced since those days. Today's wives may not be a big part of a social group. They don't always come to the games like we did. Wassermann staffs and families were a big extended family. That's why we stayed connected through all the years. Even after the Wassermanns moved to College Station, we had a few opportunities to get together and Lloyd would occasionally drop by for a surprise visit. He wouldn't often call ahead, but it was always a great surprise to be able to visit and catch up with family news.

When you need something done as a coach's wife, get ready to take responsibility to see that it gets done…unless you can wait until the end of football season, that is. We kept our households going and took care of the kids and our own job responsibilities. We also attended church, and every Sunday the Wassermanns walked in with all four kids neatly dressed. They sat in the front row on the left side, without fail.

I learned that our coaching husbands needed support in any way we could show it. It was important to be there when our husbands turned around to look for us in the stands and after the game. I remember my husband had to scout some Friday nights and would always ask me about how we scored each touchdown. We scored a LOT in some of those games, and I could never quite remember if we passed, rushed, or what!"

Janice Archer

Janice is another dear friend of the family who was great friends with my grandmother. They all shared roots in the Brenham and Nederland area, with an outlook that stretches back to the '60s! Amazingly, we are still close to this very day.

"We have known the Wassermanns since meeting them in 1966. Lloyd offered Don different positions through the years, including head baseball coach and basketball coach in Brenham. Betty was very good at attending not just the football games, but all the games. You don't see that a lot of times, but with Don being the head basketball coach, it meant a lot that Betty cheered on the basketball players too.

I remember once that both Don and I were sick, and Betty came right over and watched our little girl Donna for us. Then the whole Wassermann family came down with whatever we had!

Betty liked to talk and she never lacked for conversation. She loved tennis and played in a group. They found an instructor to teach the other coaches wives if we wanted to learn, so we'd meet and have a lesson. The instructor was very gracious, and Betty was quite a tennis player!

Lloyd and Betty moved to Nederland in the late 1970s, and we stayed in Brenham. Even though we all had separate groups of friends, we also had the closeness that our staff had developed over time. It never wavered. We would stop by and visit with Lloyd and Betty quite a few times in their home, and celebrated anniversaries, birthdays, and Lloyd's retirement.

The last time I saw Betty, she had a severe case of shingles and her son Mark was just finishing up treatment for cancer. She called me when Mark was declared in remission. When she became seriously ill, Lloyd called and asked us to put Betty on our prayer list, and we did. She was really at a point where she couldn't have visitors, but Don was in the area and saw Betty before she had her leg amputated.

We created a lot of good memories. Betty always laughed and had a smile on her face—a very congenial person. That's what I saw, and those are sweet memories. Coaches come and coaches go, but to us they were special. Lloyd and Betty were very good to us."

Epilogue

You never know what the profession will bring, but one thing is a constant—our love for our coach-husbands and our belief in the good they do.
~ **Erica Barnett**

I hope you've enjoyed this book, which published in January 2018. What a way to kick off a brand new year! Indeed, the days ahead are already busy and full of promise. I have a child to raise, a coach to support, games to cover … and a few partnerships and project announcements!

Go to Apple iTunes and download SidelinesCoach app. Also, I'm gearing up to launch the Sidelines and Pearls Coaches Wives Association—For all Sports, All Wives, Current and Retired, INCLUDING Coaches' Moms. The group motto is: *Though we may be from different coaching trees, forever united we will always be.* Be looking for that in the near future!

Oh—and there's another book on the horizon. Some coaches' wives could not be included in this book due to my publishing deadline, but I certainly want to share their insights in a sequel. So get ready for more stories, more perspectives, and more wisdom. Whether they are married to NFL, collegiate or high school coaches, each wife has something unique to share. I'll be including perspectives from coaches' moms and coaches' kids, as well, and am thrilled that these stories can be shared before they are lost to time.

So stay tuned!

~ Erica

Author's Biography

Erica Barnett has a background in nutrition and paralegal studies. She's an accomplished sports journalist and social media influencer from a sleepy Texas town called Montgomery and was born into a family tree of coaches, athletes, and sports creatives in the entertainment industry. This coach's wife, mother, daughter, and granddaughter is uniquely positioned to navigate the world of sports.

Erica blossomed by simply being "Erica." Her sideline picture with J. J. Watt at AT&T Stadium, followed immediately with a Dallas Cowboys Hype Video, elevated her sports journalism career to new levels. High school, college, NFL, MLB, and NBA teams routinely invite her to cover their games. Erica is also a motivational speaker with NFL players, a co-host on ESPN Radio, and stays busy via promos with ESPN, CBS, and USA Sports Today. She is involved in the Coaches Poll and promotes clothing lines and health & fitness products based on her background in nutrition. She is also the owner of Sidelines & Pearls and co-host and owner of The Bryan and Barnett Show.

Deeply involved in the community, she is a member of the American Football Coaches Wives Association (AFCWA), the Texas High School Football Wives Association, The Fellowship of Christian Athletes Wives Ministry, and has authored her first book, *Sidelines & Pearls: A 50-Year Perspective on the Lives of Coaches' Wives*, published January 2018. Follow her on Facebook, Twitter, Instagram and her website.

Resources

American Football Coaches' Wives Association (AFCWA)—www.afcwa.orgTexas High School Coach's Wives Association (THSCWA)—www.thscwa.org

Fellowship of Christian Athletes Coaches' Wives Ministry—fcacwm.org

Dave Campbell's Texas Football—texasfootball.com

Texas High School Football—texashsfootball.com

Old Coach FNF magazine—fnfmagazine.com/texas

Glossary

For the veteran coaches' wives, this glossary is something they've already memorized and mastered. But I decided to include it because so many newcomer wives are still learning the lingo. Hopefully, this helps break down the most common vernacular regarding players, plays, and penalties.

I think the most basic concept to master is the players. Only 11 players are on the field from one team at any one time, and each team has 3 separate units:

1.) The offense—those players who are on the field when the team has possession of the ball

2.) The defense—players who line up to stop the other team's offense

3.) Special teams that only come in on kicking situations (punts, field goals, and kickoffs).

***

1st Down (First and 10): The first in a series of four downs in which an offensive team must gain 10 yards to keep possession of the ball. If a team gains 10 yards, they are granted a first down and the right to start a new series of four downs. Depending on whether the offensive or defensive team is called for penalties, the amount of yards can be more or less than 10 yards.

3-4 Defense: A common default defensive formation called a "base defense" because it is used on 1st and 2nd downs—the "base downs."

3rd-And-Long: When the offensive team is on third down and has, usually, at least six yards to gain to get first down.

Audible: Changing the play or disguising the call to confuse or take advantage of the defense.

Backfield: The running backs and quarterback (offensive players) who line up behind the line of scrimmage.

Blitz: A defense tactic using a higher than usual number of defensive players to rush, tackle, or disrupt pass attempts by the opposing quarterback and offense.

Boxman: A person wo holds a marker signaling where the ball is, with numbers 1, 2, 3, or 4 at the top of the rod indicating which down it is.

Bull Rush: A defensive lineman attempting to plow through an offensive player rather than moving around him.

Center: The innermost lineman of the offensive line who handles the ball on every play and passes (snaps) the ball between his legs to the quarterback at the start of each play.

Cornerback: A member of the defensive backfield or secondary who lines up on the wide part of the field opposite offensive receivers to 1.) cover receivers, 2.) defend against pass offenses, and 3.) make tackles.

Defense: The team without the ball that tries to stop the offense. The 11 men on the defensive team all work together to keep the offense from advancing toward the defense's goal line.

Defensive Players: defensive tackle, defensive end, linebacker, safety, cornerback.

Delay of Game: An action which delays the game, such as the offense allowing the play clock to run out, resulting in a 5-yard penalty.

Distance: The number of yards a team needs to get a new set of four downs.

Down: A period of action starting when the ball is put into play and ending when the play is complete and the ball is ruled dead. The offense gets four downs to advance the ball 10 yards. If the offense is unsuccessful, it must surrender the ball to the opponent by punting on the fourth down.

Drive: The series of plays when the offense has the football, until it punts or scores and the other team gets possession of the ball.

Encroachment: When a defensive player crosses the line of scrimmage and makes contact with an opponent before the ball is snapped, resulting in a 5-yard penalty.

End Zone: A 10-yard-long area at each end of the field. You score a touchdown when you enter the end zone in control of the football. If you're tackled in your own end zone while in possession of the football, the other team gets a safety.

Extra Point (Point After Touchdown or PAT): A kick attempted after a touchdown, snapped to the holder from the 3-yard line (high school and college) or the 2-yard line (NFL). It must sail through the goalpost to be considered good and is worth one point.

Face Mask: When a player grabs the face mask of another player while attempting to block or tackle, resulting in a 15-yard Automatic First Down.

Fair Catch: When the player returning a punt waves his arm from side to side over his head. After signaling a fair catch, he can't run with the ball or be tackled by an opponent.

False Start: When an interior lineman on the offensive team moves before the ball is snapped, or when any offensive player makes an abrupt movement before the ball is snapped, resulting in a 5-yard penalty.

Field Goal: A three-point kick that can be attempted from anywhere on the field, but is usually attempted within 40 yards of the goalpost. This kick must sail above the crossbar and between the uprights of the goalpost.

Flea Flicker: A play in which the quarterback hands the ball off to a running back, and it's tossed back to him.

Fullback: A short-yardage runner who blocks for the running back and pass-blocks to protect the quarterback.

Fumble: Losing possession of the ball while running with it or being tackled. Members of the offense and defense can recover a fumble (called a turnover if the defense recovers the fumble).

Guard (Left Guard and Right Guard): The inner two members of the offensive line who block for and protect the quarterback and ball carriers.

Gridiron: The field of a football game looks like a gridiron (a metal grid for cooking over a fire), and this nickname has become synonymous with football.

Gunner: A special teams player who races down the field on a kickoff in or to tackle the return man.

Halfback: A running back located in the backfield.

Handoff: Giving the ball to another player, usually between the quarterback and a running back.

Hashmarks: Two rows of lines near the center of the field that are perpendicular to the side lines. Before each play, the ball is spotted between these 1-yard hashmarks, depending on where the tackle occurred in the prior play.

Helmet to Helmet Collision: When a player uses his helmet to hit into another player's helmet, resulting in a 15-yard Automatic First Down.

Holding (Defensive): When a defensive player tackles or holds an offensive player other than the ball carrier, resulting in a 5-yard Automatic First Down.

Holding (Offensive): When an offensive player uses his hands, arms, or other body parts to prevent a defensive player from tackling the ball carrier, resulting in a 10-yard penalty.

Horse Collar Tackle (banned in 2005): When football players are tackled by their necks, shoulder pads, or jerseys from behind, resulting in 15-yard Automatic First Down.

Huddle: The group of 11 players on the field who come together to strategize between plays. The quarterback relays the plays in the huddle on offense.

Incompletion: A forward pass that falls to the ground before someone catches it, or a pass that a receiver drops or catches out of bounds.

Interception: A pass caught by a defensive player, ending the offense's possession of the ball.

Kickoff: A free kick (meaning the receiving team cannot attempt to block it) that puts the ball into play. A kickoff is used at the start of the first and third quarters, and after every touchdown and field goal.

Left Tackle: One of the outer two members of the offensive line and the team's best pass blocker who often has better footwork than the right tackle in order to neutralize the pass rush of defensive ends.

Linebacker: Lined up behind the defensive linemen, they are generally the team's best tacklers who 1.) defend against the pass and 2.) push forward to stop the run or tackle the QB. Usually three or four linebackers are on the field during every play.

Line of scrimmage: An imaginary line that extends from where the football is placed at the end of a play to both sides of the field. Before the offense or the defense can cross the line, the ball must be in play again.

Moving the Ball (Run and the Pass): A play begins with the snap. At the line of scrimmage (the position on the field where the play begins), the quarterback loudly calls out a play in code and the center in front of him snaps the ball under his legs to the quarterback. The quarterback either throws the ball, hands it off, or runs with it.

Offense: Whichever team has possession of the ball is the offense. The quarterback, wide receivers, tight ends and running backs can legally handle the ball.

Offensive Backs: The three players behind the offensive line—1.) the quarterback, 2.) the fullback, and 3.) the running back.

Offensive Line: Five men who block for and protect the quarterback and ball carriers. Every offensive line has a center, two guards, and two tackles as offensive players.

Offside: When any part of a player's body is outside the line of scrimmage or free kick line when the ball is put into play, resulting in a 5-yard penalty.

Pass: Throwing (passing) the ball rather than running it. Any player on the offensive team is allowed to pass behind the line of scrimmage, although the quarterback does most of the passing. A pass is complete if the ball is caught by another offensive player, such as the wide receiver or tight end.

Pass Interference: A call made by an official when a defensive player makes contact with the intended receiver before the ball arrives, resulting in an Automatic First Down in the spot where the foul occurred.

Personal Foul: An illegal foul that risks the health of another player or causes injury, resulting in a 15-yard penalty.

Pigskin: The earliest footballs were made from natural materials like inflated pig bladders, but today are made with rubber or plastic.

Punt: The player dropkicks the ball, usually on a fourth down when the offense must surrender possession of the ball to the defense when failing to advance 10 yards.

Quarterback: The leader and playmaker who outlines each play and receives the ball from the center, hands it off to a running back, throws it to a receiver, or runs with it.

Red zone: The unofficial area from the 20-yard line to the opponent's end zone. Once the offense reaches the red zone, they are in prime position to score points.

Return: Receiving a kick or punt and running toward the opponent's goal line to gain yards or score points.

Right Tackle: One of the outer two members of the offensive line and the team's best run blocker who faces the defending team's best run stoppers. The right tackle's intent is to gain traction so the running back can find a hole to run through.

Roughing the Kicker: A defensive player makes contact with the punter (who has not yet kicked ball), resulting in 15-yard Automatic First Down.

Roughing the Passer: A defensive player makes contact with the quarterback after the quarterback has released the ball, resulting in 15-yard Automatic First Down.

Run: Occurs when the quarterback hands the ball off to a running back, who attempts to gain as many yards possible by evading defensive players. The quarterback is also allowed to run with the ball.

Running Back: A player who runs with the football, also known as a tailback, halfback, and rusher.

Rushing: To advance the ball by running rather than passing (which is why a running back is sometimes called a rusher).

Sack: When a defensive player tackles the quarterback behind the line of scrimmage, resulting in a loss of yards.

Safety: This actually has two definitions. 1.) the two points that can be scored for pinning the opposing team in their own end zone or tackling an offensive player in possession of the ball in his own end zone; 2.) a defensive player (free safety or strong safety) who is the last line of defense against the deep pass from the quarterback to the wide receiver to help stop the run.

Scoring: The game objective is to score the most points. The four ways to score points are 1.) touchdown, 2.) extra point, 3.) two-point conversion, and 4.) field goal.

Secondary: The four defensive players who defend against the pass and line up behind the linebackers and wide receivers on the corners of the field.

Shotgun: The shotgun formation spreads receivers all over the field when the quarterback takes a few steps behind the line of scrimmage in anticipation of the snap.

Snap: When the ball is hiked 1.) between the legs by the center to the quarterback, 2.) to the holder on a kick attempt, or 3.) to the punter. The ball is officially in play and action begins when the snap occurs.

Special teams: The 22 players on the field during kicks and punts, who specialize in returning and covering kicks and punts.

Tackle: The act of physically forcing (tackling) a player to the ground, or forcing one or both of a player's knees to the ground, ending the play.

Tight End: The player who blocks like an offensive lineman and catches passes like a wide receiver, lining up beside the offensive tackle to the right or the left of the quarterback.

Touchdown: A six point score earned when 1.) a player in possession of the ball crosses into the opponent's goal line, 2.) a player catches the ball in the opponent's end zone, or 3.) a defensive player recovers a loose ball in the opponent's end zone.

Two-Point Conversion: After a touchdown has already been scored, an offensive player crosses the goal line into the end zone either by running in or catching a pass in the end zone for two points, rather than kicking the extra point (one-point conversion).

Wide Receiver: A key offensive player ((AKA wideout or receiver) who 1.) catches passes in most of the passing plays, 2.) eludes defenders, and 3.) splits out "wide" near the sidelines and far away from the rest of the team. Teams use two to four wide receivers on every play.

Wildcat: The Wildcat formation calls for 1.) the quarterback to line up as a wide receiver and 2.) the running back or wide receiver to take the snap from center.

Made in the USA
Columbia, SC
27 July 2018